OCR
RECOGNISING ACHIEVEMENT

HODDER
EDUCATION

Official Publisher Partnership

OCR DESIGN & TECHNOLOGY FOR GCSE

GRAPHICS

PAUL BRANNLUND

KEVIN CRAMPTON

ANDY KNIGHT

JOHN ROLFE

EDITOR: BOB WHITE

HODDER
EDUCATION
AN HACHETTE UK COMPANY

Orders: please contact Bookpoint Ltd, 130 Milton Park, Abingdon, Oxon OX14 4SB. Telephone: +44 (0)1235 827720. Fax: +44 (0)1235 400454. Lines are open from 9.00am to 5.00pm, Monday to Saturday, with a 24-hour message-answering service. You can also order through our website www.hoddereducation.co.uk

If you have any comments to make about this, or any of our other titles, please send them to educationenquiries@hodder.co.uk

British Library Cataloguing in Publication Data
A catalogue record for this title is available from the British Library

ISBN: 978 0 340 98198 6

First Edition Published 2009
Impression number   10 9 8 7 6 5 4 3 2 1
Year   2012 2011 2010 2009

Hachette UK's policy is to use papers that are natural, renewable and recyclable products and made from wood grown in sustainable forests. The logging and manufacturing processes are expected to conform to the environmental regulations of the country of origin.

Cover photo from Don Farrall/Photodisc
Typeset by Fakenham Photosetting Ltd, Fakenham, Norfolk
Printed in Italy for Hodder Education, an Hachette UK Company, 338 Euston Road, London NW1 3BH

CONTENTS

CHAPTER 11 UNIT A534: TECHNICAL ASPECTS OF DESIGNING AND MAKING 233

ACKNOWLEDGEMENTS

The authors wish to acknowledge the help in providing exemplar coursework of the following: Mr Richard Palmer and students from Plymouth College – Michael Ashley, Lauren Auty, Amy Ballantyne, Chris Brown, Holly Champion, Natalie Chan, Sophie Collier, Sarah Deegan, Paul Huish, Zoe Lam, Oliver Mulberry, Maria Thaller, Abi Watkins and Alexandra Wooler; Mr Andy Connor and students from Severn Vale School – Sam Base, Rosie Findlater and Kayleigh Leggett; Mr Andy Knight and students from Thrybergh School and Sports College – Alaa Alnajfi, Joshua Bray, Kieran Cassin, Callum Franklin, Noura Abdul-Kadir, Jessica Lidster, Sammi Moore and Jordan Wardle.

The authors and publishers would like to thank the following for use of photographs in this volume:

Figure 2.1a Alamy/Peter Widmann; Figure 2.2 Recycle now/Graham Flack; Figure 2.3 Recycle Now/Jonathan Pollock; Figure 2.5 ASTRID & Science Photo Library; HANNS-FRIEDER MICHLER/SCIENCE PHOTO LIBRARY; Figure 2.6 Correx; Figure 2.14a © JurgaR/istockphoto.com; Figure 2.14b Alamy/STOCKFOLIO®; Figure 2.18 Roland; Figure 2.21 The Vacform Group; Figure 2.26 Versatility in Print; Figure 2.29 Alamy/Leslie Garland Picture Library; Figure 2.32 Solar Active; Figure 2.35 Alamy/imagebroker; Figure 2.36 Alamy/Mark Boulton; Figure 2.37a Paul Thompson/Corbis; Figure 2.37b © Gary Unwin – Fotolia.com; Figure 2.37c Alamy/Ken Welsh; Figure 2.38 Alamy/ImageState; Figure 2.40 GlowImages /Alamy; Figure 2.41 Getty Image/hana/Datacraft; Figure 3.7 Alamy/ICP-Traffic; Figures 3.24 and 3.25 © Crown copyright material is reproduced with permission of the Controller of HMSO and the Queen's Printer for Scotland; Figure 3.26 Reproduced by permission of Ordnance Survey on behalf of HMSO. © Crown Copyright 2006. All rights reserved. Ordnance Survey Licence number 100036470; Figure 3.50 © OCR. Reproduced with permission; Figure 3.51 © OCR. Reproduced with permission; Figure 3.53 © OCR. Reproduced with permission; Figure 3.98 Alamy/JUPITERIMAGES/Brand X; Figure 3.106 Alamy/Mike Booth; Figure 3.135 Alamy/Leo Mason; Figure 3.140 © Tony My-then 2008; Figure 3.143 Recycle Now; Figure 3.145 Alamy/Powered by Light RF; Figure 3.148 The National Association of Paper Merchants; Figure 3.155 Reproduced with permission; Figure 3.156 Alamy/Nick Hanna; Figure 4.22 © Roel Smart/iStockphoto.com; Figure 4.23 © Frank Wright/iStockphoto.com; Figure 4.24 © Stepan Popov/iStockphoto.com; Figure 4.25 ©picMax/iStockphoto.com; Figure 4.26 © Mark Kostich/iStockphoto.com; Figure 4.27 ©

Alex Slobodkin/iStockphoto.com; Figure 4.29a TechSoft Uk Ltd; Figure 4.29b TechSoft Uk Ltd; Figure 4.30a TechSoft Uk Ltd; Figure 4.30b TechSoft Uk Ltd; Figure 4.32 TechSoft Uk Ltd; Figure 4.34 Boxford Ltd; Figure 4.35 Denford; Figure 5.1 Alamy/JUPITERIMAGES/PIXLAND; Figure 5.4a Tod May/Z corporation; Figure 5.6 ©Tom Mc Nemar/istockphoto.com; Figure 5.7 Alamy/Rafael Angel Irusta Machin; Figure 5.8 PurestockX; Figure 5.9 Alamy/David J. Green – food themes; Figure 5.10b Alamy/D hurst; Figure 5.10a Alamy/SoFood; Figure 5.12a ASDA; Figure 5.12b ASDA; Figure 5.15 Alamy/Supapixx; Figure 5.16 security labels international; Figure 5.17 AlamyMBI; Figure 6.1 Alamy/Richard G. Bingham II; Figure 6.3 COSHH; Figure 7.1 Clive Tompsett; Figure 7.2 Corbis/Bettmann; Figure 7.3 Alamy/Oleksiy Maksymenko; Figure 7.6 Asus; Figure 7.8 Getty Images/David Leahy; Figure 7.10 Alamy/ImageState; Figure 7.11 ISO; Figure 7.15 Alamy/The Photolibrary Wales; Figure 9.1 Getty Images/Jody Dole; Figure 9.3 © Tye Carnelli/iStockphoto.com; Figure 9.4 © Achim Prill/iStockphoto.com; Figure 9.5 © Marcus Clackson/iStockphoto.com; Figure 9.6 © Olivier Blondeau/iStockphoto.com; Figure 9.7 © Gary Unwin – Fotolia.com; Figure 9.8 © Dawn Hudson – Fotolia.com; Figure 9.9 Fairtrade.org; Figure 9.10 © Dena Steiner/iStockphoto.com; Figure 9.12 Reproduced with permission; Figure 11.1 Alamy/Digital Vision; Figure 11.4 © OCR. Reproduced with permission; Figure 11.5 © OCR. Reproduced with permission

All illustrations in this volume by Art Construction.

Every effort has been made to trace and acknowledge ownership of copyright. The publishers will be glad to make suitable arrangements with any copyright holders whom it has not been possible to contact.

HOW TO GET THE MOST OUT OF THIS BOOK

Welcome to OCR Design and Technology for GCSE Graphics (specification numbers J303 and J043).

The book has been designed to support you throughout your GCSE course. It provides clear and precise guidance for each of the four units that make up the full course qualification, along with detailed information about the subject content of the course. It will be an extremely effective resource in helping you prepare for both Controlled Assessment and examined units.

The book has been written and developed by a team of writers who have considerable specialist knowledge of the subject area and are all very experienced teachers.

The book:
- *is student focused. The aim of the book is to help you achieve the best possible results from your study of GCSE Graphics*
- *gives clear guidance of exactly what is expected of you in both Controlled Assessment and examined units*
- *contains examiner tips and guidance to help improve your performance in both Controlled Assessment and examined units*
- *provides detailed information relating to the subject content and designing*
- *is designed to help you locate information quickly*
- *is focused on the OCR specification for GCSE Graphics*
- *has relevance and value to other GCSE Graphics courses*

The book outlines the knowledge, skills and understanding required to be successful within GCSE Graphics. It is designed to give you a 'body of knowledge' which can be used to develop your own knowledge and understanding during the course and support you when undertaking both Controlled Assessment and examined units.

Chapters 1–7 form the 'body of knowledge'. Chapters 8–11 give specific guidance about each of the units that make up the GCSE course.

▶ Unit A531 Introduction to Designing and Making

Chapter 8 gives detailed information about the structure of the Controlled Assessment Unit and the rules relating to the Controlled Assessment task you will undertake. It clearly explains what you need to do section by section and includes examiner tips to help improve your performance. Specific reference is made to the assessment criteria and an explanation is provided as to how the criteria will be applied to your product. Examples of students' work are used within the text to reinforce the requirements of each section.

▶ Unit A532 Sustainable Design

This chapter provides detailed information relating to this unit. It gives a clear explanation of the structure of the examination and gives further information relating to the key aspects of sustainability in relation to GCSE Graphics. The chapter examines:

- What we mean by the 6 R's in relation to Graphics
- The social issues governing the trends in Graphics
- The moral issues concerning Graphics
- The impact of cultural issues on Graphics
- How to select materials that are both suitable and sustainable
- Current issues affecting the design of new products

▶ Unit A533 Making Quality Products

Chapter 10 follows a similar format to Chapter 8. It explains the requirement of the unit section by section and includes examiner tips to guide you through the Controlled Assessment task.

▶ Unit A534 Technical Aspects of Designing and Making

Chapter 11 is designed to help you prepare for the written examination. It clearly describes the format of the examination paper and gives examples of questions. Examiner tips are given to help you identify the type of question and the approach you should take in completing your answer.

▶ Icons used in this book

Introduction boxes provide a short overview of the topics under discussion in the section.

KEY POINTS

- Key Points boxes list key aspects of a topic.

KEY TERM

Key Terms boxes provide definitions of the technical terms used in the section.

LEARNING OUTCOMES

Learning Outcomes boxes highlight the knowledge and understanding you should have developed by the end of the section.

EXAMINER'S TIPS

Examiner's Tips boxes give tips on how to improve performance in both the Controlled Assessment and examined units.

QUESTIONS

Questions boxes provide practice questions to test key areas of the content of the specification.

ACTIVITY

Activity boxes suggest interesting tasks to support, enhance and extend learning opportunities.

CASE STUDY

Case study boxes provide examples of how real-life businesses use the knowledge and skills discussed.

CHAPTER 1

DESIGNING AND PRODUCTION PLANNING

1.1 IDENTIFICATION OF A DESIGN NEED

By the end of this section you should have developed a knowledge and understanding of:

- the design process
- the need for a product
- what users and target markets are
- what a design brief is.

All design and technology subjects use the same design process in order to design and make products. When you are designing you will be using a wide range of both knowledge and skills. The design process illustrated in Figure 1.1 shows you the steps to follow in developing your design. You can start anywhere in the process but most people start with a design brief and end with an evaluation of their final product. You should always refer back to your specification when evaluating your final product.

Before you make a start on your design work you will need to decide on a theme for it. There is an OCR list of approved themes for each of the units of this course specification. From time to time, OCR will revise the list of approved themes for each unit, so you should always check with your teacher that you are using the current list of themes. Once you have decided on a suitable theme you will need to consider what product you could

design and make, based upon it. In making this decision you will need to think about who the **users** of your product will be, what your target market is, what the **needs** of your users are, and the **design situation** you will be designing for. Once you have all this information you should analyse it carefully. From your findings you should be able to produce a **design brief** for your proposed product.

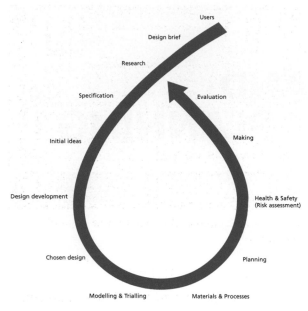

Figure 1.1 The design process

are and know what they want from the product. So you must make sure that you clearly understand who your users are. Next, look carefully at the need the users have for your proposed product, and explain it. You will then be able to write notes on a design situation, which outlines the circumstances in which the users will need the product you are intending to design.

Once you have a clear understanding of your users and their needs you should be able to present your findings and draw some conclusions. Using this information you will be able to write a design brief for your proposed product. Your design brief should be a concise statement of what you intend to design. Keep it short and try to make it a simple statement of what you are going to do.

▌ Identification of a design need

In order for any product to be successful it must have a **target market** and meet the needs of its users. The product's target market is the group of users who would want to buy or use the product you are thinking of designing. It is important that you have a clear idea who your potential users are as you must design with them in mind from the start. The list of potential users is enormous and could include any of the following:

- different age groups
- males or females, or both sexes
- a hobby or interest group
- different businesses or industries
- public service organisations or different charities.

The key thing is to identify who your users

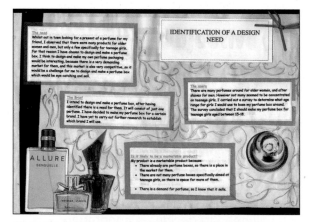

Figure 1.2 Lauren's 'identification of a need' worksheet

Examiner's comments

- Lauren has clearly stated both the need and the users of her proposed product.
- Her small survey of users has helped her to understand their needs.

- Her design brief is both clear and concise.

- The border and additional illustrations are not required at this stage and would not gain her any extra marks.

- The information provided would easily have fitted on a quarter of a sheet of A3, thus avoiding an unnecessary waste of valuable portfolio space.

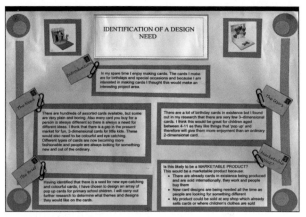

Figure 1.4 Sophie's 'identification of a need' worksheet

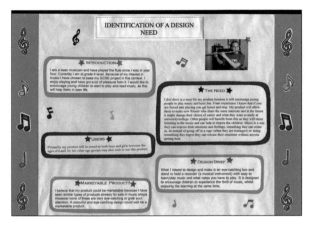

Figure 1.3 Maria's 'identification of a need' worksheet

Examiner's comments

- Maria has explained her design situation. She has identified the need for her product but her reference to users is a little limited.

- Her design brief is clear and concise.

- The illustrations are unnecessary and would not gain her any additional marks.

- Better use of space would have resulted in this information being presented in a much smaller area.

Examiner's comments

- Sophie explains clearly both the need and users of her proposed product. She has also identified her design situation.

- The initial survey of potential users has helped her understand their needs.

- Her design brief is both clear and concise.

- However, she does not explain the target market very precisely and greater detail is required here.

- This section was presented over two pages of A3. The border and additional illustrations will gain her no extra marks, and the information could have been presented on half a sheet of A3, saving valuable portfolio space.

KEY POINTS

You need to:

- clearly identify the users of your proposed product
- clearly identify the needs of your users
- clearly identify your target market
- clearly state your design situation
- write a concise design brief for your proposed product.

EXAMINER'S TIPS

You should:

- remember the product is not for you, so try to work closely with your users
- edit your findings so as to include only relevant information about your users, their needs and the target market
- make sure that your design brief is a short and clear statement; avoid writing too much detail into your design brief – a couple of sentences is all that is required
- keep your design brief realistic – you *must* be able to make the product; your design brief should be sufficiently 'open' so as to give you scope for design; it should provide you with the opportunity to demonstrate your designing skills; do not forget to mention the intended users and the target market.

KEY TERMS

DESIGN BRIEF – short, clear statement of what you are going to design
DESIGN SITUATION – the circumstances in which users will use the product
NEED – why users require the product
TARGET MARKET – group of users
USERS – people who will use the product

▶ Your checklist

Have you:

- chosen a theme from the current approved OCR list
- identified the users
- identified your target market
- described a design situation
- identified the need for your proposed product
- analysed your findings
- edited your work – removing any irrelevant information
- presented your work in a logical manner
- produced a design brief that
  - is realistic
  - is 'open' (allows you to design 'outside the box')
  - will lead to a quality product
  - mentions both users and needs?

▶ Portfolio requirements

For Unit A531: 1 × A3 sheet or equivalent

ACTIVITY

1. (a) Working in pairs, select a theme from the current OCR list.
   (b) List all the products you could possibly make using this theme as a starting point.
   (c) Next, individually, select one product from your list and identify potential users and why they need the product. Then compare your list of users and needs with your partner's.

2. (a) The pop-up card has been a highly successful product for the greetings card market. Identify the various users of pop-up cards and explain what needs the product has satisfied.
   (b) Write a design brief for a pop-up card for a birthday greeting. Try to include reference to both users and needs in your design brief.

) 1.2 ANALYSING A DESIGN BRIEF

LEARNING OUTCOME

By the end of this section you should have developed a knowledge and understanding of:

- how to analyse a design brief.

*Your design brief should be a short, clear statement of what you intend to design and make. However, it does not tell you very much about the project you are about to undertake. To find all the information you will need in order to proceed with your project, you will have to **analyse** your design brief. To do this you will need to ask yourself and others a lot of questions about your proposed product. Once you have the answers to these questions you will be better placed to complete your research.*

) Analysing a design brief

Analysing your design brief involves asking questions to find out exactly what you should design and make. A good way of doing this is by asking Who, What, Where, When, Why and How questions about your proposed product. For example:

- *Who* are your users and your target market?
- *What* has the product got to do?
- *Where* will it be used?
- *When* will it be used?
- *Why* is it needed?

- *How* will it be made? *How* much will it cost? *How* many are needed?

Figure 1.5 Sophie's analysis of her design brief

Examiner's comments

- Sophie asks a lot of questions on her design brief, which will guide the direction of her research.
- This worksheet is well presented and visually interesting but it has used far too much space.

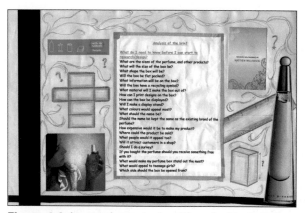

Figure 1.6 Lauren's analysis of her design brief

Examiner's comments

- Lauren asks herself a lot of questions about her design brief. She has used the Who, What, Where, When, Why, How method very well.

- This thorough analysis will ensure that she takes her research in the right direction. However, the analysis could have been presented on half a page.

KEY POINTS

Remember:

- by analysing the design brief, you will identify the information that you need to gather in order to help develop your design
- use the Who, What, Where, When, Why, How method to analyse your design brief.

EXAMINER'S TIPS

You should:

- always analyse your design brief fully as this will help you to identify the most useful information you need in order to develop your design ideas
- be selective – use only information that is relevant to your proposed product
- be concise (to the point) in the information you include in your design folio, and explain why it is useful.

KEY TERM

ANALYSE – to examine critically so as to identify the most important aspects of the design brief

▶ Your checklist

Have you:

- explained who your users are
- explained the needs of your users
- explained what your product has to do
- identified where your product will be used
- explained why your product is needed
- identified how your product will be made, and how many are required
- understood your deadlines?

▶ Portfolio requirements

For Unit A531: 1 × A3 sheet or equivalent

For Unit A533: 1 × A3 sheet or equivalent

ACTIVITY

1. *Design brief:* Design a secure packaging system to promote sales of a webcam attachment for a laptop computer. From this design brief you are to identify:
    - a range of users
    - what the product has to do
    - where it will be used
    - why it is needed
    - how it will be made.

2. *Design brief:* Design a logo for a sports equipment manufacturer which specialises in water sports. From this design brief you are to identify:
    - a range of users
    - what the product has to do
    - where it will be used
    - why it is needed
    - how it will be applied.

1.3 EXISTING PRODUCT ANALYSIS

LEARNING OUTCOMES

By the end of this section you should have developed a knowledge and understanding of:

- how to analyse an existing product
- how to identify trends in existing products
- how to use the information you find out in your design work.

Gathering information about existing products is a great way to develop an understanding of the existing market, what products exist already and what you will be competing against. Most good designs come about through improving upon existing designs. Developing your understanding of existing designs will help you to produce a good design.

Analysing existing products

In order to find out as much as you can about existing products you will need to:

- photograph them before and during use
- draw and sketch them
- measure them
- identify all the materials used
- identify the **production methods** used
- identify the **assembly methods** used
- **disassemble** them – to see how they are formed, made, joined
- note any graphics on the product, including mandatory information
- identify any laws or regulations that apply to the product
- consider their good and bad points
- seek the opinions of users
- identify how they satisfy user needs.

You probably need to analyse at least two existing products in detail to get a full understanding. Try to be selective with the information you present, using only that which will directly help you with your design

work. Explain clearly and in some detail what you have found out about the existing products you select. You will also need to consider any trends in the development of existing products. Trends occur when designers seek to match each other's designs in order to maintain the interest of the users. A good example of this is the Dyson 'Cyclone' vacuum cleaner, which was a unique concept when first produced; now all major manufacturers offer a similar product. So, when you are analysing existing products, try to identify the trends that have influenced their design.

When you have gathered and presented your information on existing products you will need to consider how this information can help you with your design work. You will need to ask yourself some questions. For example:

- What have you learnt from looking at them?
- How will the good and bad points you have found influence your design?
- What features of each existing product could be useful in your design?

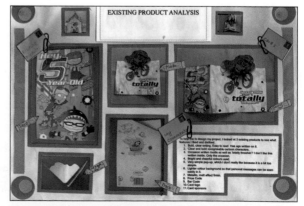

Figure 1.7 Part of Sophie's analysis of existing products

Examiner's comments

- Sophie has shown her chosen existing product from different angles using full-size originals and copies.
- The analysis is fairly thorough but lacks references to the size of the product and details of the 'pop-up' mechanism.

Examiner's comments

- Holly has used photographs to illustrate the existing product. There is some analysis but it could have been further improved by including precise details of how the hands are fixed and rotate, together with full measurements of the clock body.

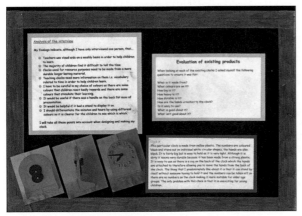

Figure 1.8 Part of Holly's analysis of existing products

EXAMINER'S TIPS

You should:

- avoid simply describing the obvious things about existing products; try to show that you are making judgements, analysing and evaluating
- use drawings and sketches to explain your thoughts and opinions
- ensure that your analysis of two existing products in detail will be sufficient to score maximum marks
- avoid simply cutting and pasting lots of examples of existing products – concentrate on examining just a few existing products in detail
- make a list of the trends you find in existing products.

KEY TERMS

ASSEMBLY METHODS – the way in which the product is put together
DISASSEMBLE – to take the existing product apart in a controlled way
PRODUCTION METHODS – the way in which the product is made

KEY POINTS

Remember to:

- examine a minimum of two existing products in detail
- clearly explain what you have found out about your existing products, and show how this information could influence your design work
- identify the trends that have influenced the design of the existing products.

▶ Your checklist

Have you:

- identified the materials used in the existing product
- identified the production and assembly methods used
- disassembled your existing product
- stated the good and bad points of the existing products
- identified why the existing products do, or do not, satisfy the needs of users
- drawn or sketched the existing products, including their important measurements
- identified trends in existing products?

▶ Portfolio requirements

For Unit A531: 2 × A3 sheets or equivalent

ACTIVITY

1. Select one of the following iconic products: Dyson vacuum cleaner; Mini; Coca-Cola bottle; Heinz Tomato Ketchup bottle; Barbie doll; Chanel No. 5; Lego building bricks.
   (a) Identify all the good and bad points of the design, and explain why the product appeals to users so much.
   (b) Consider ways in which the product could be improved.

2. For this exercise you will need a thin cardboard package like that in which toothpaste is sold.
   (a) Disassemble it carefully. Note how the development (net) is folded and assembled. How are the end flaps held in place after the product has been put inside? What method is used to keep the package together?
   (b) List the information and graphics that appear on the outside of the package. Identify any information on the package that you think might be mandatory.

3. Mobile phones are an essential product for many people. Identify the current trends in mobile phone design.

1.4 IDENTIFICATION OF COMPLEX ASSOCIATIONS LINKING THE PRINCIPLES OF GOOD DESIGN AND TECHNOLOGICAL KNOWLEDGE

LEARNING OUTCOME

By the end of this section you should have developed a knowledge and understanding of:

- what is meant by the complex associations linking the principles of good design and technological knowledge.

▶ Complex associations linking the principles of good design with technological knowledge

The **principles of good design** may require a graphic product to be functional, aesthetically pleasing, sustainable and strong, yet lightweight. Our use of **technological knowledge** helps us to understand the properties of materials: how they can be cut, shaped and formed; how they can be joined together; how they can be finished. So, in order to produce a good-quality product, you must have an understanding of how you can combine the principles of good design and technological knowledge into a workable solution.

For example, if you were designing a 'blister' plastic package to contain an MP3 player, in addition to considering the design requirements of the package you would need to have a good knowledge of thin sheet plastics. You would need to find out which ones are best suited to vacuum forming. You would also need to know the properties of the materials and their limitations, as well as what equipment you have available. You would need to find out how large a vacuum forming you could make and how big a mould the vacuum former could take. Only by combining

an understanding of these critical elements would you be able to produce a design that had a good chance of being successful.

KEY POINT

Remember:

- all designers must have an understanding of the principles of good design, and be able to combine it with the technological knowledge needed to produce a workable product.

EXAMINER'S TIPS

You should:

- always be realistic in your approach to design as it is better to succeed with something you are able to complete rather than embark on a project that you have little chance of finishing
- check that your proposed product is achievable using the materials and equipment available
- aim to design a practical working product.

KEY TERMS

COMPLEX ASSOCIATIONS – the intricate way in which things are linked
PRINCIPLES OF GOOD DESIGN – the factors that determine whether a design is successful
TECHNICAL KNOWLEDGE – the understanding of graphic materials and processes

▌ Your checklist

Have you:

- demonstrated an understanding of the complex associations linking the principles of good design with technological knowledge, as outlined in the Creativity section of Unit A531?

ACTIVITY

You are planning to design and make an educational pop-up book for young children. Identify the principles of good design and technological knowledge that will influence your design work.

1.5 RESEARCH, DATA AND ANALYSIS

LEARNING OUTCOMES

By the end of this section you should have developed a knowledge and understanding of:

- how to carry out different types of research
- how to present the data you have gathered
- how to analyse the data.

Research is the process of finding out information. As you gather the information it should be analysed to determine how relevant it is to your design project. You should ensure that you continually add to your research throughout your design project – it should not simply be done at the beginning and not returned to. You should explain the relevance of any new information you have added as your project develops.

▶ Research, data and analysis

There are several different types of information you can use. Information based on facts is called **objective information**. When the information you use is based on an opinion and not on facts it is known as **subjective information**. Information that can be collected directly from the situation by, for instance, asking users for their opinions is known as **primary research**, whereas information that can be found in sources like books or from the internet is called **secondary research**.

Primary research

This type of research involves activities such as:

- visits
- surveys
- interviews
- using questionnaires
- taking photographs.

Primary research is a very good method of collecting information as it makes you, the designer, find out for yourself exactly what the problems and issues are from the point of view of users of the products.

Visits and interviews

You may wish to visit your users and record their views about an existing product. Through observation of them using existing products and asking them questions you will be able to determine what they expect from the product. You may also wish to interview experts who have knowledge of existing products or the design problem you are working on. You will need to record any useful advice they have.

Surveys and questionnaires

These are an effective way of gathering information from a lot of users or potential users. The key to success when using surveys and questionnaires is to ask the right questions. Make sure you list all the information you need to find out about your potential product, then devise questions that will get the answers you need from users. So, if you were planning to design a travel game, you might consider asking users the following questions.

- What type of game appeals to you?
- How long would you play for?
- Would you share the board or prefer one each?
- What method of random selection would you prefer (e.g. dice/spinner)?
- What size game would you prefer?
- What type of game (e.g. chance, skill, knowledge, strategy)?

Taking photographs

Take photographs of users with existing products and in the situation in which they may use your proposed product. It is useful to annotate the photographs to explain their relevance.

Secondary research

This type of research involves you looking at the work of other people. You can collect secondary research from such sources as:

- books and magazines
- the internet
- CD-ROM
- published expert opinion
- libraries/museums

- manufacturers
- retailers.

The amount of secondary information that will be available to you is enormous, so you will need to be very selective. Only include information that has clear relevance to your design product. Try to avoid including too much information just because you have gathered a lot.

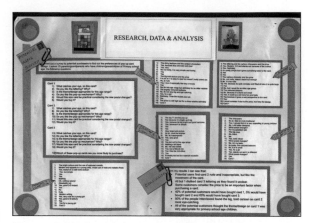

Figure 1.10 Sophie's survey of potential users of pop-up cards

- Her questions are well thought out and should provide her with appropriate information.
- She has recorded her findings and then very precisely reported her conclusions.

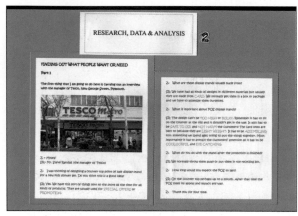

Figure 1.9 Zoe's interview with a user of her proposed product

Examiner's comments

- Zoe has visited a local supermarket to speak with the manager about her product.
- The result of this brief interview with someone who has a lot of experience of point-of-sale display has given Zoe some very useful information about her product – good primary research.

Examiner's comments

- Sophie has carried an interesting survey of a small sample of potential users.

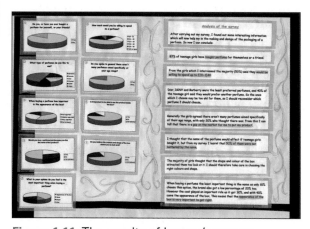

Figure 1.11 The results of Lauren's survey

Examiner's comments

- Lauren has used a computer package to aid the presentation of the findings of her research with a series of pie charts (questionnaire on a separate page).

- She then draws some very clear conclusions from her research, which are well presented.

▶ Data presentation

Your research will involve you in collecting data. This data will be mostly in written form. In your portfolio you should present your data visually. You can do this using:

- tables
- line graphs
- bar charts
- pie charts
- pictographs.

Tables

If you are using questionnaires or surveys as a means of gathering information, you will need to put together all the information you have found. Tables are a very good way of showing graphically the answers to each question or the results of your survey.

Line graphs

Line graphs usually have a horizontal and vertical axis. They are useful for showing the relationship between two factors, such as the sales figures of a company shown rising or falling over time.

Bar charts

Bar charts usually have a horizontal and vertical axis. Information is shown as a series of bars the same width with a gap in between each bar. The bars can be drawn either horizontally or vertically.

3D bar charts are far more visually interesting as they are drawn in three dimensions – good for showing information like the monthly

maximum temperature of a holiday location in a travel brochure.

Pie charts

A pie chart is a diagram where the whole is represented as a circle. The circle is then divided into sectors to represent the information as a proportion or percentage of the whole. Pie charts can also be drawn in three dimensions for greater visual impact.

Pictographs

Pictographs are based on the same principle as a bar chart but use a pictorial symbol instead of a bar to shown the statistical information. They are visually interesting and very easy to understand. They are good for showing information like the sales of motor cars across Europe.

Once you have completed your research and presented it in your portfolio you will need to analyse it and summarise your findings. This can be done using 'bullet point' statements

KEY POINTS

Remember:

- there are two types of research – primary (what you can find out for yourself) and secondary (what you find out from the work of others)
- objective information is based on facts
- subjective information is based on opinions
- you must explain the relevance of the information you have gathered
- you must draw conclusions from your research.

that explain what you have found out, how the information is useful to you and how it will influence your design.

EXAMINER'S TIPS

You should:

- make sure the information you present is relevant to your product; be selective with your choice of information to be included in your work – you will need to explain why you have used the information otherwise it will not add to your marks
- always include a conclusion to your research; explain what you have found out and how it will help you in your design work.

KEY TERMS

OBJECTIVE INFORMATION – information based on facts

PRIMARY RESEARCH – information you have found out for yourself

SECONDARY RESEARCH – information that is the work of others or based upon images

SUBJECTIVE INFORMATION – information based on opinion

Your checklist

Have you:

- planned your research
- stated the needs of users
- used both primary and secondary research
- edited your research and presented only relevant material
- drawn conclusions from your research that will help you develop your design?

Portfolio requirements

For Unit A531: 1 or 2 × A3 sheets or equivalent

ACTIVITY

Imagine you are going to design a three-dimensional restaurant menu.

(a) Consider the possible sources of information on restaurant menus.
(b) Identify potential users and make a list of information you will need from them.
(c) Draft six key questions, to go in a questionnaire, that you will ask your users.

1.6 DEVELOPING A DESIGN SPECIFICATION

By the end of this section you should have developed a knowledge and understanding of:

- what a design specification is
- how to develop a design specification
- how to present your design specification.

Once you have completed your research, you must draw detailed conclusions from all the information you have collected. You can then use your conclusions as a guide when writing your design specification.

Developing a design specification

Your design **specification** is a checklist that you should refer to throughout the design and making of your product. By continually referring back to your specification you will ensure that the focus of your design is always centred on meeting the needs of the users of the product. The word specification comes from the word 'specific', so remember as you write your specification to make it clear and precise. Try to avoid using vague statements like 'strong', when producing your specification. Remember that if your product needs to be strong then you should provide a more detailed explanation as to why strength is a requirement.

Specifications could include any of the following criteria.

- **Purpose**: what is it meant to do – what is its function?

- **Aesthetics**: how will colour, shape, form, texture and/or pattern influence the design?

- **Ergonomics/anthropometrics**: how will the design affect the user – what data on humans will you require for this design?

- **Quality control**: how will you ensure consistent quality?

- **Target market**: who are the users of the product?

- **Moral issues**: concerning the rights and wrongs of human behaviour.

- **Cultural issues**: how different cultural backgrounds, religions and lifestyles may influence the design.

- **Social issues**: the influences that society might have on the design.

- **Environmental issues**: the increasing influence that care for the environment has on design.

- **Safety**: what safety factors need to be considered?

- **Size/weight**: specific size/weight/strength issues.

- **Materials**: what qualities are required of the material?

- **Type of production**: for the quantity required.

- **Regulation**: what laws or regulations apply to the product?

- **Product life cycle**: for how long has the product got to last?

- **Reliability/performance**: how will you ensure the product works as intended, and what is the tolerance level before failure occurs?

- **Cost**: will the product be designed to a fixed budget?

You will need to select the criteria that apply to your proposed product. Then you should write a brief statement containing the detail of how each of the criteria will apply to your product. For example, when designing a pop-up greeting card you may decide that its size is important. This might lead you to state that there is a requirement for the final design to fit in an A5-size envelope.

Figure 1.12 Lauren's design specification

Examiner's comments

- Lauren has produced a very thorough specification, which covers the key criteria in considerable detail.

- This will provide an excellent checklist to refer to as she develops her product.

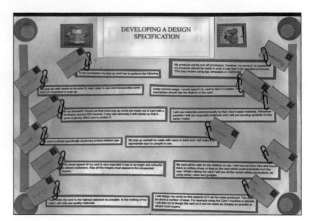

Figure 1.13 Sophie's design specification

Examiner's comments

- Sophie has produced a very concise design specification. It covers all the key criteria in detail.

- It will provide a very useful checklist to refer to as the design develops.

- The over-elaborate presentation, however, would not score her any additional marks.

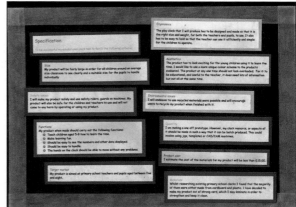

Figure 1.14 Holly's design specification

Examiner's comments

- Holly has produced a very clear and concise design specification.
- It covers all the key criteria for her educational clock in detail and will be a very useful checklist to refer to as the product design develops.

You should present your specification as a series of bullet points, with each of the criteria having precise details of the expected requirements.

You may wish to prioritise your specification under three headings, as follows.

1. *Must*: essential features of the product.
2. *Should*: desirable features of the product.
3. *May*: optional features of the product.

KEY POINTS

Remember:

- your specification is a checklist that will be referred to throughout the design project
- your specification needs to be clear and concise
- to make sure you have included all the criteria that are relevant to your proposed product.

MUST	SHOULD	MAY
Display product/information Be interesting Be eye-catching Attract buyers Be stable Be functional Flat pack for ease of transport Have bold clear message/lettering Be lightweight yet strong Occupy a specified space Be easily assembled Assemble without glue Have a limited life span Be freestanding or fit on a counter top Limited budget Be single colour Have no sharp corners/protruding features	Original Be recyclable Occupy a specified surface area Be made of environmentally friendly materials Flat pack to specific size Be two colour	Be unique Be reusable Be full colour

Figure 1.15 An example specification for a point-of-sale display

EXAMINER'S TIPS

You should:

- always write your specification as a series of bullet points
- aim to produce a clear, concise specification – one that accurately states what it is that you are designing
- ensure that all the relevant criteria have been included, and explain why each is important
- ask yourself if anyone reading your specification for the first time would have a clear understanding of what it is that you intend designing and making; if the answer is no, then you will need to add further details to your specification
- always use a computer to produce your specification, then it can be easily reproduced as required throughout the unit.

KEY TERMS

AESTHETICS – the look of the product (elegance, shape, form)

ANTHROPOMETRICS – data on human sizes

ERGONOMICS – how it relates to the human form (e.g. holding, carrying)

QUALITY CONTROL – how you ensure consistent quality (accuracy of production)

REGULATION – what rules and legislation apply to this product

SPECIFICATION – list of features your intended product should have; each is a performance target that your product should meet and will be evaluated against

Your checklist

Have you:

- selected and edited the information
- analysed your findings
- produced a design specification that:
  - is detailed
  - focuses on your product
  - uses bullet points
  - avoids vague terms
  - shows structure and priorities
  - has been saved using ICT so that it can be retrieved, reviewed and revised throughout the design process?

Portfolio requirements

For Unit A531: 1 × A3 sheets or equivalent

For Unit A533: 1 × A3 sheets or equivalent

ACTIVITY

1. Write a specification for your mobile phone.

2. Imagine you have been asked to design a new, recyclable bottle for Coca-Cola. List the criteria you would include in a specification for this new product.

3. A package is to be designed to securely display a pair of energy-efficient light bulbs. List the criteria you would include in a specification for this package.

1.7 GENERATING IDEAS AND COMMUNICATING DESIGN

By the end of this section you should have developed a knowledge and understanding of:

- how to present your ideas
- how to analyse your ideas
- how to identify your chosen product outcome
- how to test your ideas
- how to present your final design.

You now need to communicate and explain your ideas. You should present your ideas using a variety of communication techniques. You should aim to produce a broad range of ideas. All your ideas should be evaluated against the product specification. You should then choose the idea, or combination of ideas, that best meets your specification to develop into a product.

▌ Generating ideas

You should start with quick freehand sketches of your initial ideas. These should be both 2D and 3D sketches in pencil or ink. Alternatively, you may wish to use ICT to help you generate your initial ideas. Both freehand and computer methods are equally acceptable. Always annotate your sketches to explain your ideas. Make sure you include all your ideas: not just those you consider to be good but also those you are unsure of, or those that you think have weaknesses. It is important to show that you are thinking about

your design in the broadest sense at this stage. This is often referred to as 'thinking outside the box'. Keep referring back to your specification to keep your design focused. Try to make sure that you record and include all the sketches of and notes on your ideas, even those drawn on scraps of rough paper. It is quite acceptable to cut and paste them into your presentation.

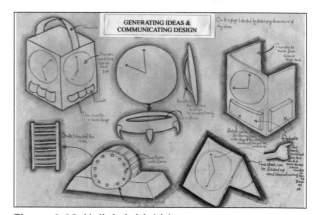

Figure 1.16 Holly's initial ideas

Examiner's comments

- Holly has produced a very good worksheet of initial ideas (this being the first of two) with eight ideas in total.

- Her sketches are bold and easy to understand. There is good use of annotation around her sketches, which further helps to explain her ideas.

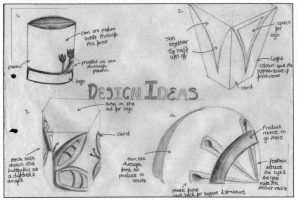

Figure 1.17 Rosie's initial ideas for a perfume package

Examiner's comments

- Rosie has produced sketches of her initial ideas for perfume packages.

- The sketching is bold and clear, with annotation to explain her ideas.

- With better use of space Rosie could have included all her initial ideas on this one page.

- The full analysis of each idea is contained on a later worksheet.

Once you are satisfied that you have a broad range of ideas, you should evaluate them. In order to evaluate your ideas you will need to reference each one against your design specification to measure their strengths and weaknesses. You should note how well each idea meets each of the criteria of your specification. You can present these evaluations either as a series of written notes adjoining the sketches of each idea, or by producing a table to show how you have evaluated all your ideas against your design specification. Once you have evaluated all

your ideas you will be in a position to identify the idea, or combination of ideas, that you intend to develop for your product. You should always state very clearly why an idea has been chosen to be developed further.

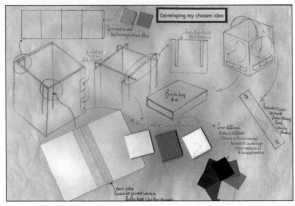

Figure 1.18 Holly's development of her ideas

Examiner's comments

- Holly has provided good details of a number of ways she might construct her product.

- The worksheet contains information on proposed materials, construction and joining methods.

- Again, the sketching is precise and clear, and this makes it very easy to understand her ideas.

▌ Product development

Product development is the process whereby you transform your chosen idea into a marketable product.

To ensure you complete a successful product outcome you will need to carry out the following steps as part of your product development:

- Combine the best parts of your ideas.

- Improve and refine your ideas.

- Carry out further research, especially into production methods.
- Make choices about materials (see Section 1.10).
- Produce models and mock-ups to test your ideas.
- Evaluate against the product specification as you go.
- Investigate how the product will be made and assembled.
- Design an appropriate control system, if required (e.g. jig, template, mould, CAD/CAM).
- Produce a presentation and scaled drawing of your product.

Modelling and mock-ups

You will need to test your ideas to see if they work. You can do this either by using materials like paper and card to physically make test models and mock-ups, or you can use a CAD package to model your ideas on the computer. (See Section 1.8 for more details.)

Control systems

The type of product you intend to make will determine whether you need a control system within the making process. **Control systems** can provide better-quality control and accuracy of production, and enable you to produce a batch of your product. Jigs, templates, moulds and the use of CAD/CAM are all examples of control systems.

Presentation and scaled drawing

Once you have completed the development of your idea, it is important to produce two key drawings of your product. First, a pictorial drawing (often referred to as an artist's impression) of what your completed product will look like when finished; this is usually a 3D drawing, in **isometric or perspective drawing** with colour and rendering added. Second, a scaled drawing (known as a working drawing) in **third-angle orthographic**, which shows different views of your product and has all the relevant dimensions applied. (See Chapter 3 for more details on these types of drawings.)

Examiner's comments

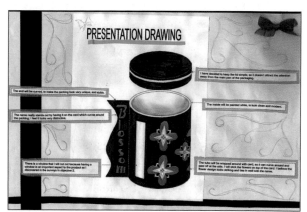

Figure 1.19 Lauren's artist's impression of her prototype product

- Lauren has produced a very good 3D artist's impression of her product.
- She has annotated her drawing to provide additional information about her design.

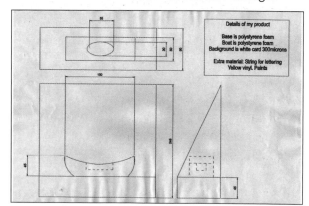

Figure 1.20 Zoe's third-angle orthographic drawing of her point-of-sale stand

Examiner's comments

- Zoe has used a computer package to produce this third-angle orthographic drawing of her countertop point-of-sale display stand.
- The drawing should include details of its scale.

Examiner's comments

- This working drawing has some component sizes missing.
- It also fails to show exactly where the components fit in to the layout of the pop-up card.
- It would be better to concentrate on the parts of the card in the working drawing, and provide a separate drawing to show how the colour and graphics would be applied.

KEY POINTS

Remember to:

- produce lots of quick freehand sketch ideas, or use ICT to produce your initial ideas
- add notes around your sketches to explain how your ideas work
- include all your ideas, not just the ones you consider good
- evaluate your ideas against your design specification
- clearly explain reasons for your choice of idea to develop
- fully test your ideas using modelling and trialling techniques
- produce presentation and scaled drawings of your proposed product.

Figure 1.21 Sophie's working drawing of her pop-up card

EXAMINER'S TIPS

You should:

- present a wide range of ideas using a variety of presentation techniques, from freehand sketches through to ICT work using CAD
- include a wide range of ideas that are clearly different – not simply cuboids with different graphics
- explain your ideas clearly and in detail – do not assume the examiner will understand; check with others to see if they understand what you are doing
- add brief notes around each sketch to fully explain your ideas
- add extra sketches and notes to explain design detail
- use quick, simple sketches to explain your ideas – avoid works of art
- remember that colour and rendering are not essential for 'initial idea' drawings
- always explain fully to the examiner how you are developing your product – use sketches and notes to show any changes and modifications you make
- include a control system to ensure product quality
- explain to the examiner how the product might be produced in quantity
- produce a 3D artist's impression of your product; use colour and rendering to enhance your drawing
- produce a dimensioned scaled orthographic drawing of your product that you can use to work from as you make your product.

KEY TERMS

CONTROL SYSTEMS – used to ensure accuracy and quality of production
ISOMETRIC/PERSPECTIVE DRAWING – a method of drawing in 3D
THIRD-ANGLE ORTHOGRAPHIC DRAWING – a method of drawing in 2D

▶ Your checklist

Have you:

- presented a range of ideas in sketch form
- designed 'broadly'
- explained fully each idea
- evaluated each idea – using the specification as your checklist
- explained your choice of idea to product-develop
- provided the evidence and results of modelling and testing your ideas
- explained how your product will be made
- explained what your product will be made of
- explained how your product will be assembled
- explained what control system you are using to ensure a quality product
- explained what processes you will use
- checked your ideas against the product specification
- produced an artist's impression and scaled drawing of your product?

▶ Portfolio requirements

For Unit A531: 2 × A3 sheets or equivalent

For Unit A533: 3 × A3 sheets or equivalent

ACTIVITY

1. Sketch freehand design ideas for a set of signs for a leisure centre. Use as few words as possible in your ideas.

2. Produce a presentation (artist's impression) drawing of your mobile phone.

3. Draw in third-angle orthographic three views of a closed laptop computer, then add dimensions to your drawing.

1.8 MODELLING AND TRIALLING TECHNIQUES

LEARNING OUTCOMES

By the end of this section you should have developed a knowledge and understanding of:

*   how to model and trial your ideas.

Modelling and trialling are essential parts of the development of your product. You can use the compliant materials for this specification in your modelling, or you can use ICT to computer-model your ideas.

Modelling and trialling using models and mock-ups

It is important that you test your ideas using models and mock-ups. These can be made of paper, card or any other appropriate material. They will help you to understand how your product will look in 3D, how it will fit together, and what type of fastenings or fixings you will need. You will also be able to test the appropriateness of the material you intend to use. Do not forget to record the findings of all your tests and explain how they

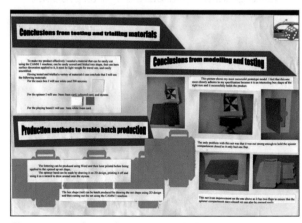

Figure 1.22 One of Amy's modelling worksheets

will influence your design. Make sure that you take photographs of your models, or keep the models and mount them flat in your folder, then annotate them to explain their purpose.

Examiner's comments

*   This worksheet provides evidence of Amy's modelling and trialling of her ideas using card mock-ups.

- Her comments tell us what she has learnt from her modelling and the modifications she has made to her net design.

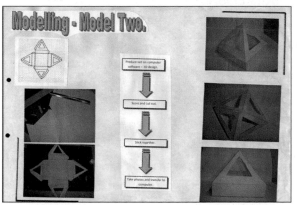

Figure 1.23 Kayleigh's modelling of her perfume packaging

Examiner's comments

- Kayleigh has used 2D design to produce her model.
- Evidence of her modelling is provided by the photographs.
- Kayleigh has provided comments and analysis of her model on the next page in her portfolio – it would have been better included on this page.

▶ Modelling and trialling using CAD and CAM

If are able to use a CAD package to model your ideas, remember that it is just another tool to help you with your design work, so the software package you have available is not that important. What is important is that the CAD work you produce is of good quality and appropriate. It is very easy to spend a lot of time on the computer trialling your ideas without having anything to show for it. So it is vital that you save the CAD work as you go along. Then, later on, you can print off some

screenshots to provide evidence of the modelling and trialling you have done for your portfolio.

Figure 1.24 One of Lauren's modelling pages

Examiner's comments

- Lauren provides photographic evidence of her modelling and trialling.
- By annotating the photographs she has explained in detail what she has learnt from her models.
- The use of colour and graphics helps her decide on the suitability of her ideas.

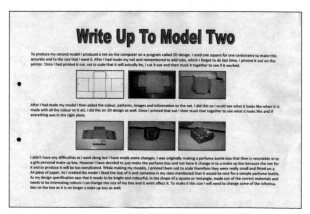

Figure 1.25 Sam's modelling of her perfume package

Examiner's comments

- Sam has used 2D design to produce the initial net of her package.

- The photographs record the modelling she has undertaken.

- Initial models and those with graphics included are shown.

- Sam fully explains the modelling and trialling, and explains the problems she experienced and how they were solved.

KEY POINTS

Remember to:

- use models and mock-ups to test your ideas

- explain fully the outcome of your modelling and trialling

- evaluate your ideas against the product specification

- keep all the evidence of your modelling and trialling.

KEY TERM

SCREENSHOTS – pages taken from your modelling using CAD

▶ Your checklist

Have you:

- used test models to develop and test your ideas

- provided evidence and recorded the findings of your modelling and trialling?

▶ Portfolio requirements

For Unit A531: 2 × A3 sheets or equivalent

For Unit A533: 4 × A3 sheets or equivalent

EXAMINER'S TIPS

You should:

- provide evidence of modelling, which can be the models themselves or photographs of the models; if you use ICT, then print off some screenshots as examples of the computer modelling you have undertaken; explain what you have done, using notes and labels.

- make sure you include all the evidence of the modelling and trialling you have carried out; very often candidates leave this out of their portfolio, which means no marks can be awarded – so keep the evidence to show how your product developed!

1.9 DIGITAL MEDIA AND NEW TECHNOLOGIES

By the end of this section you should have developed a knowledge and understanding of:

- digital media and new technologies.

Digital technology has allowed us to transfer information at great speed in text, visual and audio formats. The internet provides us with the online ability to carry out research. CAD and CAM applications are now used extensively in schools and colleges.

▶ Digital media and new technologies

CAD (computer-aided design) systems could include:

- computer
- graphics tablet
- scanner (flat or 3D)
- internet access

- 2D or 3D software.

CAM (computer-aided manufacture) systems could include:

- computer
- CNC lathe, miller, router
- laser cutter
- 3D printer
- plotter/cutter, vinyl cutter.

You can use computer systems to carry out 2D and 3D modelling of your ideas. They provide you with the ability to rotate your ideas to see them from numerous different angles. You can zoom in to see fine detail or zoom out to see the overall effect. You are able to change colour, texture and graphics easily until the desired combination is found. It also means that you have the ability to make modifications easily and speedily.

1.10 MATERIAL SELECTION

By the end of this section you should have developed a knowledge and understanding of:

- how you are going to make your prototype product
- how to make key choices about the materials you are going to use.

At this stage in the design process you are going to have to make some important decisions.

- *What materials are available to you?*
- *Which materials are best suited to your prototype product?*
- *How are you going to make your prototype?*

▌ Material selection

You will need to find out a lot more about the materials you are likely to use in your product.

- What materials are available in your school or college?
- What materials are appropriate for your prototype?
- Some materials may need to be ordered so you will need to check delivery times.
- Will the availability/cost/suitability of materials lead to compromises in your design?

You will need to test the suitability of the materials you are considering using. This may require you to use models to test the appropriateness of the material – will the material do what you want it to do?

When testing materials you must record your findings and explain your reasons for selecting particular materials. The following are the types of tests you will need to perform and the types of information you will need to find out.

- How well does the material fold, score and cut?

- Does it take colour from paints or inks, and/or can it be printed on?
- How can it be joined together – does it take glues or adhesives, or will you need to use alternative fixing methods?
- What tools or processes can be used with particular materials?
- Are any health and safety issues raised by the materials you have tested?

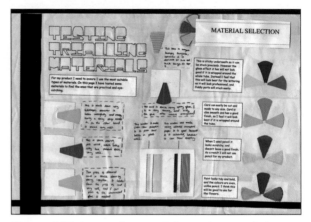

Figure 1.26 Lauren's materials testing worksheet

Examiner's comments

- Lauren has tested different adhesives.
- She has also assessed how each material take colour finishes.
- She has explained her choice of material.

Figure 1.27 Maria's materials testing worksheet

Examiner's comments

- Maria has explained her choice of material in depth.
- She explains her choice of fastenings.
- She mentions that she will be making a blister pack but gives little detail of the plastic sheet she intends to use.

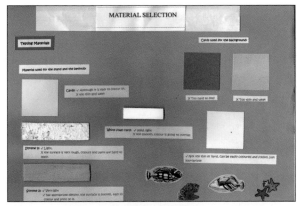

Figure 1.28 Zoe's materials testing worksheet

Examiner's comments

- Zoe's presentation of her materials looks visually impressive.
- She could have provided far greater detail

on her reasons for choosing and rejecting materials.

You should present the results of materials tests using notes and sketches, or in chart form. Any models used in the tests should be photographed, or the tests themselves could be photographed at different stages to show what you have done.

Once you have completed all your testing you will need to clearly identify the materials you feel are suitable for your prototype product and explain the reasons for your choice.

KEY POINTS

Remember to:

- identify suitable materials that are available in your school or college
- test each material to see how appropriate it is for what you want it to do
- keep detailed records of all your tests
- explain the reasons for your choice of materials.

EXAMINER'S TIPS

You should:

- know that making an appropriate choice of material is an essential ingredient in producing a high-quality prototype product
- be aware that the area of material testing and analysing is one that is frequently under-researched by candidates.

▌ Your checklist

Have you:

- identified all materials, tools and equipment you intend to use, and justified their use
- tested the materials suitability through modelling, then recorded your findings
- tested all joining methods and recorded your findings
- considered how many are required and how you will control the quality of the product

- designed, made and tested any jigs, templates or moulds you intend to use
- highlighted any health and safety issues concerning your choice of materials, tools and equipment?

▌ Portfolio requirements

For Unit A531: 1 × A3 sheets or equivalent

For Unit A533: 1 × A3 sheets or equivalent

◗ 1.11 PRODUCTION PLANNING

LEARNING OUTCOMES

By the end of this section you should have developed a knowledge and understanding of:

- the importance of good planning
- how to plan the production of your project.

It is essential that you produce a detailed plan of exactly how you are going to make your proposed product. Without careful planning your chances of successfully producing a high-quality product outcome will be very limited.

▌ Production planning

There are a number of different aspects to your planning that you will need to present, as outlined below.

- *Time:* you will need to plan your use of time very carefully, particularly as each project will have a fixed time allowance –

20 hours. To ensure you score maximum marks it is essential that you complete all aspects of the project to the deadline set by your teacher. A Gantt chart (see below) offers a very good way to plan the efficient use of time.

- *Materials:* make a detailed list of all the materials you are going to need. Make sure you include the **dimensions** (length × width × thickness) of every piece of material. You will also need to check that the materials you require are available.

- *Pre-manufactured components:* you will need to give details of any **pre-manufactured components** (e.g. fastenings, fixings) you will be using, and again it is important to check their availability.

- *Tools/equipment/processes:* you will need to list all the tools and equipment you intend to use. You will need to identify the processes you are going to use, including any uses of CAD.

- *Risk assessment:* it is important that you identify in your planning any health and safety risks in the making process.

- *Health and safety:* you must show that you can work safely, and it is very important that all health and safety issues are identified in your planning.

Once you have identified all these aspects of your project plan you can decide on the order of work that you are going to follow. It is important to show that you have a logical sequence in which to make your product. You must include every stage of making in your planning.

You can use a variety of methods to present your planning:

- Gantt charts (see Figure 1.29) are good for time management planning

- block diagrams can be used to show materials and components

- flow charts and annotated storyboards are good for showing the process and sequence of making.

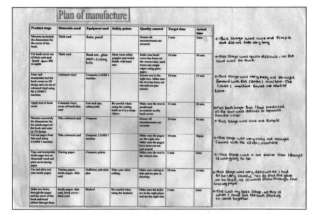

Figure 1.30 Sarah's plan of manufacture of her educational clock

Examiner's comments

- Sarah has used a table to present her manufacture plan.

	Hours	1	2	3	4	5	6	7	8	9	10	11	12	13	14	15	16	17	18	19	20
Creavity	Predicting	▓	▓	▓																	
	Actual	▓	▓	▓	▓																
Designing	Predicting				▓	▓	▓	▓	▓	▓											
	Actual					▓	▓	▓	▓												
Making	Predicting										▓	▓	▓	▓	▓	▓	▓	▓			
	Actual													▓	▓	▓	▓	▓	▓		
Evaluation	Predicting																			▓	▓
	Actual																		▓	▓	▓

Figure 1.29 Gantt chart showing the planning of Unit A531

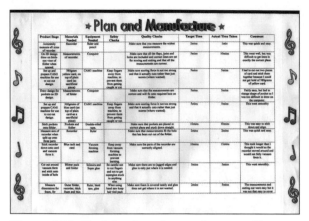

Figure 1.31 Maria's plan of manufacture of her recorder presentation pack

- She has added handwritten comments on how the making has progressed. These will prove very useful when she comes to the evaluation of her product.

Examiner's comments

- Maria has used a table to present her manufacture plan. Her comments are thorough and detailed.

- The comments on how the making has progressed will be very useful to her when she comes to the evaluation stage.

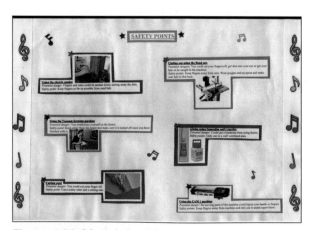

Figure 1.32 Maria's health and safety issues

Examiner's comments

- Maria has presented a number of health and safety issues in the making process of her educational clock.

- She also suggests appropriate precautions.

- She has used far too much space for the presentation of her work.

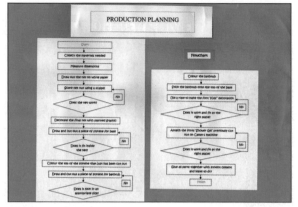

Figure 1.33 Zoe's flow chart of her production plan

Examiner's comments

- Zoe's flow chart clearly identifies the different stages in the production of her countertop point-of-sale display unit.

- It shows that she has thoroughly planned her production.

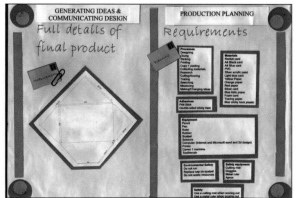

Figure 1.34 Sophie's planning requirements

Examiner's comments

- Sophie has presented a large amount of information on this worksheet. However, it could be improved by providing both the sizes and the amount of each material that is required.

- The health and safety and risk assessment aspects also need to be more detailed.

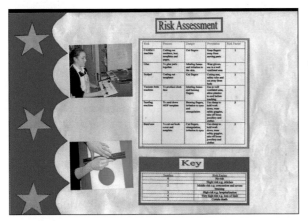

Figure 1.35 Sarah's risk assessment

Examiner's comments

- Sarah has carried out an appropriate risk assessment, which has been well presented using a table.

Once you have produced your making plan it is important to record on it, by adding brief notes, how the making task progresses. You should keep a diary of any problems or changes you experience while making your prototype, as well as showing how well you have used the time available. This information will prove invaluable to you when you come to write your evaluation of your product and its making.

KEY POINTS

Remember:

- the key to completing a successful, high-quality product outcome is detailed and careful planning

- to keep a diary of the making process of your product as this will help you with your evaluation.

EXAMINER'S TIPS

You should:

- always produce your plan before you start making – examiners are very good at spotting plans that have been written later
- make the purpose of your plan to be an aid to meet deadlines and produce a high-quality product
- keep a diary of the making process (e.g. use of time, problems and changes)
- use a range of presentation techniques to show your production planning.

KEY TERMS

DIMENSIONS – the measurements of materials used

PRE-MANUFACTURED COMPONENTS – components that you have bought in, not made yourself

Your checklist

Have you:

- included a time plan to help you meet deadlines
- added notes to record progress
- kept a diary of the making process
- produced a materials list, including all dimensions
- identified all pre-manufactured components you intend to use
- listed all tools, equipment and machines you intend to use, and how you will use them

- listed and described all the processes you will use, and how you will use them
- explained the use of CAD/CAM in your work
- carried out a risk assessment
- identified all health and safety issues
- produced an order of work and recorded progress using a storyboard?

Portfolio requirements

For Unit A531: 2 or 3 × A3 sheets or equivalent

For Unit A533: 2 or 3 × A3 sheets or equivalent

1.12 CRITICAL EVALUATION SKILLS

LEARNING OUTCOMES

By the end of this section you should have developed a knowledge and understanding of:

- the importance of critical evaluation skills
- how to produce a critical evaluation
- what should go into a critical evaluation
- how the critical evaluations are different for Unit A531 and Unit A533.

In Unit A531 your critical evaluation will focus on the making process for your prototype product, whereas in Unit A533 the focus of your critical evaluation will be the graphic product you have made.

Unit A531 Introduction to design and making: critical evaluation

This final part of the design process requires you to evaluate the processes involved in making your product model and ask the following questions of it.

- How well did the making process go?
- How well did you use the time available?
- What problems did you experience making your prototype?

- What changes were made to the making process?
- What modifications to the making process could you suggest to improve it?

Critical evaluation

The best source of information for this critical evaluation will be the diary you have kept during the making process. You should approach this task with honesty, highlight things that went well but, equally, be critical of things that went wrong. You will receive credit for both types of comment if you support them with evidence. Your evaluation should include a report on the making process of your prototype. You should discuss each stage of the production of your prototype. Focusing on how well the making went, you should include any problems you experienced in making your prototype and how they were overcome. You should discuss your management of the time available and highlight any processes that took longer than you had planned for. In your report you should identify any changes you made to the making process and give your reasons for the changes. You should then complete your evaluation by suggesting future modifications that could be made to the making process.

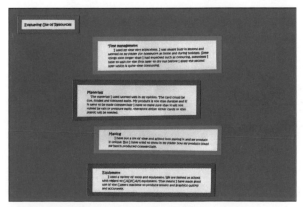

Figure 1.36 Zoe's evaluation page

Examiner's comments

- Zoe has provided a very brief evaluation of the making process.
- Each of the identified areas needs far greater depth of explanation.
- Problems and changes need to be explained and details provided on how they were overcome – she should refer back to her diary of the making process for the details.

KEY POINT

Remember:

- for Unit A531 your critical evaluation should focus on the making process.

EXAMINER'S TIPS

You should:

- always try to complete your evaluation – it is the section most frequently left unfinished by candidates
- refer back to your production diary for any changes you made to the making process
- focus your evaluation on the making process – changes, problems and future modifications.

▶ Your checklist

Have you:

- reviewed your making diary and identified any changes or problems

- suggested future modifications, using sketches and notes
- presented your evaluation concisely and logically?

Portfolio requirements

For Unit A531: 2 × A3 sheets or equivalent

Unit A533 Making quality products: critical evaluation

This final part of the design process requires you to test your finished product and ask the following questions of it.

- *Does it do what you intended it to do?*
- *Does it meet the needs of users?*
- *Does it satisfy the design brief?*
- *Does it meet the product specification?*
- *How can it be improved?*

Critical evaluation

You will need to start your evaluation by referring back to your original design brief – how well does your prototype product satisfy it? You need to be honest and praise your successes, but equally you should be critical of any failings in the product. Provided you back up your statements with evidence you will be rewarded for both positive and negative comments about your product. Now check your product specification and compare each point to see how well your product has done. You will need to explain any changes you have made to the design either during development or when you were making it. Be precise in describing the changes and explain why you made them. Your production diary is often a good source of information about changes, as long as you have recorded them!

Your evaluation should include the following information.

- How well the materials you chose performed.
- How well the tools, equipment and processes you used worked.
- How well you managed the time available for the project.
- Testing with *real* users – record their opinions, likes/dislikes and any improvements they suggested.
- All the evidence of your testing; this can include questionnaires, interviews and records of conversations, charts/tables, photographs and the opinions of experts.
- Suggestions for modifications and improvements to your product. You may also wish to highlight any issues that remain unresolved.

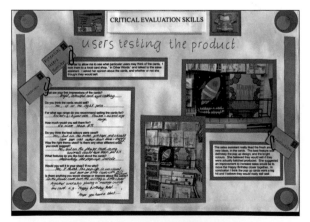

Figure 1.37 Sophie's 'user' testing page

Examiner's comments

- Sophie has taken her cards to a card shop to seek the opinions of users (the sales assistants who sell cards).

- She had prepared a questionnaire for her users.

- She makes a few minor suggestions for modifications – a more detailed explanation of the outcome of her testing and possible modifications is required.

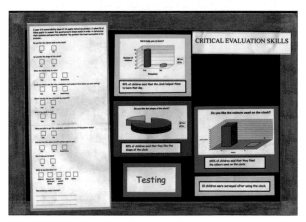

Figure 1.38 Holly's interview with a teacher

Examiner's comments

- Holly took her educational clock into a school to test it with the children and their teacher.

- She carried out a survey with 34 children, who all used the clock.

- She then interviewed the teacher using well-structured questions.

- Using both the survey results and the answers from the interview, she was able to draw some conclusions, and identify both successes and areas for modification.

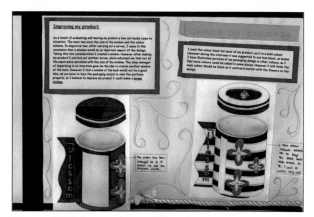

Figure 1.39 Lauren's modifications page

Examiner's comments

- Lauren has used the comments she gained from testing with the users of her product to identify problems for modification.

- She has proposed modifications, which she has illustrated well.

- She could have used space on the page better – half a sheet of A3 should be sufficient.

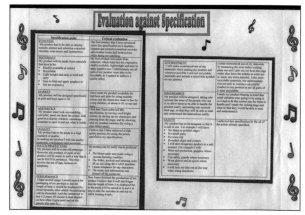

Figure 1.40 Maria's evaluation against her specification

Examiner's comments

- Maria has produced a very detailed evaluation against her specification.
- She takes each of the specification criteria in turn and explains both the successes and a few problems she encountered.

KEY POINT

Remember:

- for Unit A533 the critical evaluation should focus on the finished product with particular reference to the specification, detailed testing and proposals for modifications.

EXAMINER'S TIPS

You should:

- always try to complete your evaluation – it is the section most frequently left unfinished by candidates
- test and evaluate your prototype product – this should *not* be a record of *your* performance in the project
- refer back to your production record for any changes you made
- evaluate the control system you used – its performance, problems and how it could be improved
- always test your product on actual users; record their honest opinions, and always avoid simply using friends or family for the tests.

▶ Your checklist

Have you:

- compared your final product with your final product specification – point by point?
- reviewed your production diary, and identified and explained any changes?
- reviewed your use of materials, tools and equipment?
- tested your product on users?
- reviewed your system of control (e.g. jigs, templates, moulds); could they be improved?
- suggested future modifications, using sketches and notes?
- presented your evaluation concisely and logically?

▶ Portfolio requirements

For Unit A533: 2 or 3 × A3 sheets or equivalent

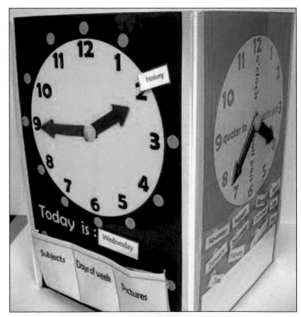

Figure 1.41 Holly's educational clock

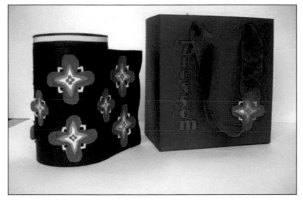

Figure 1.42 Lauren's perfume packaging

Figure 1.43 Maria's recorder presentation pack

Figure 1.44 Sarah's educational clock

Figure 1.45 Zoe's point-of-sale display unit

CHAPTER 2

MATERIALS

2.1 CLASSIFICATION OF GRAPHIC MATERIALS

By the end of this section you should have developed a knowledge and understanding of:

- the range of materials used in graphics
- the classification of materials used in graphics.

*There is a very wide **range** of materials available for designing and making. In graphics we tend to use sheet material, such as card, and block material, such as Styrofoam™. These can be combined to create models and prototypes.*

Materials used in graphics

Paper

Paper is perhaps the most common material used in graphics. Paper is a thin material that is mainly used for writing, drawing and printing on, but it can also be folded to make three-dimensional objects. It is produced by pressing together moist fibres – typically cellulose pulp derived from wood – and drying them into flexible **sheets**.

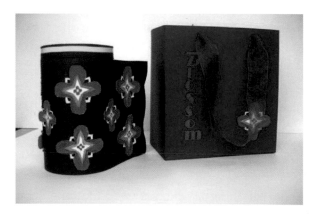

Figure 2.1 Models and prototypes

Paper is available in many different sizes, weights and finishes, but can broadly be **classified** as:

- recycled paper, which contains a minimum of 75% genuine waste; the waste might be printed or unprinted waste paper collected from offices or households

- virgin fibre paper, which has never been used before by a manufacturer to make paper or other products.

Figure 2.2 Paper

Cardboard

Cardboard is a general term for a heavy-duty (thick or strong) paper-based material. Cardboard products can be recycled, as long as they are not laminated with another material. The fibres that make up cardboard get shorter each time they are pulped, which means that cardboard can be recycled only four or five times before the fibres disintegrate.

Cardboard is available in many different sizes, thicknesses and finishes, but can broadly be classified as:

- corrugated cardboard, which is often used in packaging

- flat cardboard, which is used to make such things as cereal packets.

Figure 2.3 Cardboard

Foam board

Foam board is a lightweight board made from polystyrene foam sandwiched between sheets of paper or card. It is available in a variety of sheet sizes, colours and thicknesses (5 mm-thick board is the most popular). Foam board is commonly used for display work and model making. You should always test an adhesive before using on foam board as some adhesives contain polystyrene solvents, which will melt polystyrene.

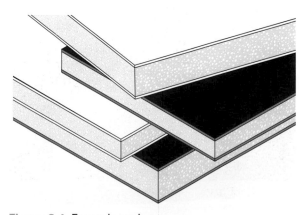

Figure 2.4 Foam board

Plastic sheet and sections

Plastic is a general term for a wide range of synthetic materials made from oil. Plastics are classified as:

- thermoplastics, such as PVC
- thermosetting plastics, such as urea-formaldehyde.

Thermoplastics become soft when heated and can therefore be shaped by vacuum forming or blow moulding. Thermosetting plastics do not become soft when heated and are chemically set, or cured, once they have been formed into a shape. Most plastics can be recycled or reused.

Plastics are available in many different types, colours and forms (sheet, block, section, rod and tube). A section is a shaped strip of material (e.g. a U section or an L section). The most common types of plastic used in graphics are PVC, polypropylene, acrylic and self-adhesive vinyl.

To be fully compliant with this specification the plastic sheet used in the making of products should be no more than 1mm in thickness.

Figure 2.5 **Plastic**

Corriflute

Corriflute is an **extruded** corrugated plastic sheet produced from high-impact polypropylene resin. It is a lightweight material, which can be cut easily with a craft knife.

Corriflute is commonly used to create signs, such as those used by estate agents, and for constructing plastic containers and packaging. Corriflute is recyclable and is therefore considered by many to be environmentally friendly.

Figure 2.6 **Corriflute**

Styrofoam™

Styrofoam™ is a general term for expanded polystyrene foam. It has a small, closed-cell structure that is easily shaped and sanded to provide a smooth surface. It is available in a wide range of sheets and **blocks**, and is often used in packaging and modelling.

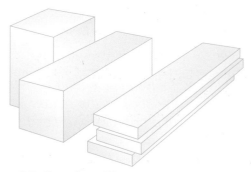

Figure 2.7 **Styrofoam™**

KEY POINTS

The main materials used in graphics are:

- paper
- cardboard
- plastic sheet and sections
- corriflute
- Styrofoam™.

These materials can be classified, or sorted, into groups. For example, plastics can be either thermoplastics or thermosetting plastics.

EXAMINER'S TIP

The best way of developing a good working knowledge of the range of materials used in graphics is to use them in your designing and making tasks.

KEY TERMS

BLOCK – material that has a thickness greater than 10 mm
CLASSIFICATION – sorted into groups
EXTRUDED – material shaped by forcing through a die
RANGE – breadth or scope
SHEET – a thin piece of flat material (less than 10 mm)

2.2 PERFORMANCE CHARACTERISTICS OF GRAPHIC MATERIALS

LEARNING OUTCOME

By the end of this section you should have developed a knowledge and understanding of:

- the performance characteristics of materials used in graphics.

*A key factor in selecting a material for a specific purpose is the **performance** characteristics of the material. Performance **characteristics** can be divided into physical properties and aesthetic qualities.*

▶ Physical properties

Physical properties are those features of a material that can be measured or tested. It is, therefore, possible to compare one material with another (e.g. PVC sheet is harder than Styrofoam™). The five physical properties of a material you should consider are as follows.

Hardness

Hardness is the ability of a material to resist pressure (not easily scratched or dented). In terms of graphic materials, acrylic sheet is considered to be relatively hard and foam board relatively soft.

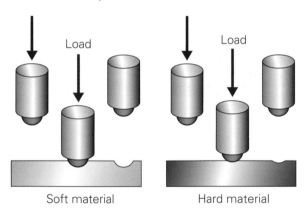

Soft material   Hard material

Figure 2.8 Hardness

Toughness

Toughness is the ability of a material to absorb energy (an impact) and deform

Figure 2.9 Toughness

(change shape) without fracturing (snapping). In terms of graphic materials, self-adhesive vinyl is considered to be tougher than acrylic sheet.

Flexibility

Flexibility is the ability of a material to flex, or bend, time and time again. In terms of graphic materials, paper is more flexible than foam board.

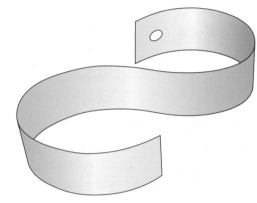

Figure 2.10 Flexibility

Strength

There are two types of strength, as described below.

Compressive strength

Compressive strength is the ability of a material to withstand pushing or squashing forces. If a material is being squashed it is said to be 'in compression'. When the limit of compressive strength is reached, materials are crushed. Concrete has a high compressive strength.

Tensile strength

Tensile strength is the resistance of a material to a force trying to pull it apart. If a material is being pulled apart it is said to be 'in tension'. String has good tensile strength but very little compressive strength.

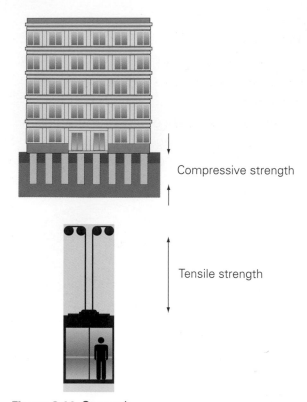

Figure 2.11 Strength

Strength to weight ratio

Strength to weight ratio is the specific strength of a material divided by its density (weight). It is expressed in newton metres per kilogram, and is used to calculate tensile strength and compressive strength. Materials with very high specific strengths, such as aluminium and titanium alloys, are widely used in aerospace applications where weight savings are more important than material costs.

▌ Aesthetic qualities

The term 'aesthetic qualities' refers to the appearance of a material. This cannot be tested or measured as easily as physical properties, and has much more to do with user feelings or perceptions. The three aesthetic qualities of a material you should consider are as follows.

Colour

Colour is the appearance of an object in terms of hue (e.g. red, yellow, blue), lightness (e.g. pastel, vivid) and saturation (how close it is to grey). Most materials are available in a wide range of colours. Colour selection will have a huge impact on the appearance of a product (consider, for instance, the same item of clothing in two different colours).

The colour wheel (Figure 2.12) is used to show the primary, secondary and tertiary colours. Colours that are next to each other on the colour wheel are said to be in harmony (sit together well) and colours that are opposite are said to be contrasting (strikingly different).

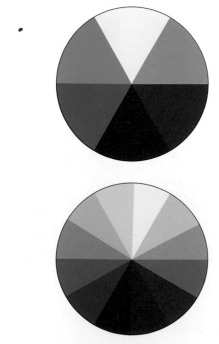

Figure 2.12 The colour wheel

Texture

Texture is either the feel or look of the surface of a material. A surface can be textured (rough to the touch) or rendered to look textured (the surface is smooth but the surface graphics makes it look rough). For example, a plastic laminate used to make furniture might look textured for aesthetic reasons but may actually be smooth so that it is easier to clean.

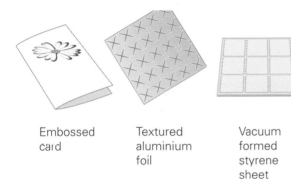

Embossed card

Textured aluminium foil

Vacuum formed styrene sheet

Figure 2.13 Textured surfaces

Surface finish

Surface finish is largely concerned with whether a material is gloss or matt, although there are lots of different finishes in between (e.g. eggshell, sheen, lustre). A shiny surface reflects light, while a matt surface does not.

KEY POINTS

The performance characteristics of a material you should consider are as follows.

- Physical properties:
  - hardness
  - toughness
  - flexibility
  - strength
  - strength to weight ratio.
- Aesthetic qualities:
  - colour
  - texture
  - surface finish.

EXAMINER'S TIP

Make sure you consider the performance characteristics of a range of materials before justifying the selection of a specific material.

Gloss photograph

Figure 2.14 Surface finishes

Matt photograph

KEY TERMS

AESTHETIC QUALITIES – user perceptions or feelings towards a material

CHARACTERISTICS – features or attributes of a material (they can usually be measured or tested)

PERFORMANCE – how well a material works, or functions

PHYSICAL PROPERTIES – actual characteristics used to identify or describe a material

QUESTIONS

1. Consider the physical properties a material needs to have if it is to be used to make a bag to carry shopping.

2. Use the colour wheel to justify the selection of colours for the background and images on a safety sign.

2.3 FORM AND SELECTION OF GRAPHIC MATERIALS

LEARNING OUTCOMES

By the end of this section you should have developed a knowledge and understanding of:

- the forms in which graphic materials are available
- how the forms of materials available will affect selection.

*Graphic materials are available in a wide range of different **forms**, such as sheet, block and tube. You will need to understand the forms in which each material is available before you can **select** a specific material.*

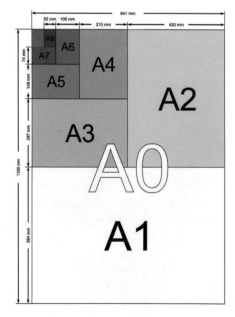

Figure 2.15 Common paper sizes

▶ Forms of material

Paper

Paper is available in sheets and rolls of different size, weight and finish. The majority of paper is purchased in sheet form (common sizes are A3 and A4) and in reams (500 sheets of paper).

Paper weights are quoted in grams per square metre (gsm). Standard photocopying paper is usually 80 gsm.

Paper is either coated or uncoated. Most of the paper used in laser printers, duplicating machines and on commercial print jobs is uncoated. Paper that is coated is used for high-quality printing and is good for reproducing photographs. The most common coated paper has a glossy finish. It is often used for catalogues and slick brochures.

You will significantly reduce the purchase cost and amount of waste if you use standard-size sheets of paper for print runs.

Cardboard

Cardboard is available in sheets of different sizes, thickness and finish. The term card tends to refer to the thinner material (as used for greetings cards), and the term cardboard to thicker material (as used to mount prints). Corrugated card is also available in rolls and sheets.

The size of the sheets of cardboard varies enormously so it is a good idea to do an internet search to find the most appropriate size for a particular task.

The thickness of card and cardboard is usually measured in microns (1000 microns = 1 mm). The card used in graphics usually ranges from around 200 microns to 1000 microns. Card is sometimes described in terms of how many sheets of paper thick it is. For example, a 240 micron card may be known as '3-sheet'.

Cardboard is usually over 1000 microns in thickness. Cardboard is available in a variety of different finishes, colours and textures. Thicker cardboard is relatively expensive so

you must not only choose the correct size but also the correct thickness if you are to avoid unnecessary expense.

Foam board

Foam board is available in sheets of different sizes, thickness and colour. The most common sheet sizes are A1 to A3. Common thicknesses of foam board sheet are between 3 mm and 10 mm, with perhaps 5 mm the most commonly used. Foam board is usually white but other colours, including black, are available.

Plastic sheet and sections

Plastic sheet and sections are available in many different sizes, colours and materials. You should always try to use standard sizes as this will reduce the cost of purchase and the amount of waste. An internet search will give you a very good idea of what is available. Make sure you also choose the correct material for your particular use. For example, polyethylene is tough at low temperatures, with excellent chemical and electrical insulation properties. Acrylic can be completely transparent and will not discolour or degrade under UV light.

Corriflute

Corriflute is available in sheets of different sizes, thickness and colour. The most common sheet size is 610 mm × 610 mm. The most common thickness for corriflute sheet is 4 mm. Corriflute is usually purchased in packs of mixed colours that contain red, blue, white, yellow, green and black sheets.

Styrofoam™

Styrofoam™ comes in sheets and blocks of different sizes and thickness. A common sheet size is 600 mm × 1200 mm, with thicknesses between 25 mm and 100 mm.

The colour is either pale blue or pink, but this is unimportant because Styrofoam™ is often painted after shaping. If you are using Styrofoam™ to make a concept model you can reduce waste by gluing offcuts together to make the correct-size block.

KEY TERMS

FORM – types available, such as sheet size or colour
SELECT – to choose

KEY POINT

The materials used in graphics are available in many different forms. A quick internet search will give you a good idea of the range for a specific material. You should make a selection based on what you need to make your design. It will be wasteful to buy sheets of material that are considerably larger or thicker than you require.

QUESTIONS

(a) Use the internet to research the forms in which corriflute is available.

(b) Produce an order for the corriflute required to make 100 signs (each sign is 300 mm × 300 mm and can be in any colour).

(c) Calculate the total cost of your order and estimate the cost of any waste.

EXAMINER'S TIP

Never use a material without being able to justify why you have chosen the material. You should have considered the forms the material is available in and the working properties.

2.4 CONVERSION OF GRAPHIC MATERIALS

LEARNING OUTCOMES

By the end of this section you should have developed a knowledge and understanding of:

- ways of converting graphic materials into other useable forms
- safety precautions that should be observed when converting materials.

Conversion of a material means to turn it into another useable form. The three main ways of converting graphic materials are by:

1. cutting
2. forming
3. combining or joining.

▶ Cutting

Cutting is the most common way of converting a material into another useable form. For example, large sheets of card can be cut into smaller pieces.

Sheets of paper and cardboard can be cut with scissors, a craft knife, rotary trimmer or guillotine. A craft knife should always be used with a safety rule and a cutting mat. A guillotine should always be fitted with a safety guard.

Specialist cutting equipment such as a circle cutter (like a compass but with a blade instead of a pencil) and a perforation cutter (cuts a 'dashed' line) are commonly used in graphics.

Sheets of foam board can be cut with a craft knife. You will not achieve a clean cut through polystyrene (it will tend to crumble or break away) unless you use a sharp craft knife. By cutting part-way through foam board the bottom layer of card can be used as a hinge.

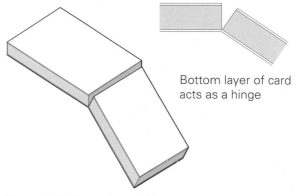

Bottom layer of card acts as a hinge

Figure 2.17 Foam board hinge

Plastic sheet and sections can be cut with a craft knife, saw or CNC machine, such as a vinyl cutter. CNC machines will allow you to very quickly cut out a large number of **identical** shapes.

Figure 2.16 Craft knife, safety rule, cutting mat and guillotine

Figure 2.18 Vinyl cutter

Corriflute can be cut with a craft knife. Corriflute is easy to cut when cutting parallel to the inner walls and more difficult to cut when cutting through the walls. This can present problems when cutting out a circular shape.

Figure 2.19 Cutting corriflute

Styrofoam™ can be cut with a craft knife or a hot wire cutter. If the craft knife is not sharp, the Styrofoam™ will crumble, leaving an unsightly edge. A hot wire cutter will give a much cleaner cut, but suitable **extraction** methods should be available as the **fumes** can be harmful.

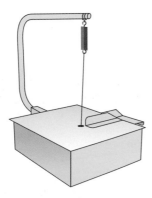

Figure 2.20 A hot wire cutter

▶ Forming

Forming is a means of turning a flat sheet of material into a three-dimensional form. For example, a polystyrene sheet can be vacuum formed to make a tray. Other methods of forming sheet material are line bending and blow moulding.

Figure 2.21 A commercial vacuum forming machine

▶ Combining or joining

Combining materials means to join them together so that they form a single material. For example, paper can be laminated (combining paper and polyester) to form a new material that is tougher and waterproof.

Figure 2.22 A commercial laminating machine

KEY POINTS

The three main ways of converting graphic materials are by:

1. cutting
2. forming
3. combining or joining.

It is important to use the correct tools or equipment to convert a material and observe any safety precautions that will ensure your personal safety.

KEY TERMS

CONVERSION – changing a material from one form to another
EXTRACTION – method of removing
FUMES – vapour or smoke
IDENTICAL – the same

EXAMINER'S TIP

Exam questions will focus on naming the tools or equipment required to convert a material, and ways of ensuring your personal safety.

QUESTIONS

(a) Name the tools or equipment you would use to convert an A3 piece of card into six rectangles that are 80 mm by 200 mm.

(b) Explain why you would not use an A2 piece of paper to cut out the six rectangles.

2.5 FINISHING PROCESSES APPLIED TO GRAPHIC MATERIALS

LEARNING OUTCOME

By the end of this section you should have developed a knowledge and understanding of:

* methods of finishing graphic materials.

Finishing processes that are applied to graphic materials are usually things that are done to a sheet of material after it has been printed. The finishing processes described in this section are:

* *laminating*
* *varnishing*
* *embossing*
* *foiling*

- *die cutting and stamping*
- *folding*
- *collating*
- *binding.*

It is unlikely that you will use all these finishing processes on a single product, but you will need to understand how they are done and the effect they will have on the physical properties or aesthetic qualities of the material. In industry these processes are **automated** *to deal with high volumes of production but most can be* **replicated** *in a school situation.*

Finishing processes

Laminating

Laminating is the process of applying a film to either one or both sides of a printed document. Laminating a printed document will:

- add lustre or gloss

- provide strength

- make the document waterproof, tearproof and tamperproof.

Laminating can be a useful addition to posters, membership cards, menus, signs, photographs, badges and certificates. Laminating films are available as a pouch or in a roll.

Laminating films in pouch form are like envelopes and are sealed on one edge. They come in many sizes to accommodate items such as letterheads and business cards. A3- and A4-size laminating pouches are readily available in schools.

Laminating films on a roll are either applied to the front side of a document or the document is sandwiched between two layers of film. Rolls of laminating film are commonly used in

a commercial setting where high-volume runs are required.

Both forms of laminating film are available in various thicknesses and finishes. The three main materials used for the laminating processes are polyester, polypropylene and nylon.

The two main methods of laminating are:

1. thermal laminating

2. cold laminating.

The material used for thermal laminating consists of a laminating film and an adhesive. The adhesive is dry and not tacky to the touch. The document is placed between the two layers of the laminate film (often a pouch) and then sent through equipment (a laminator) where the dry adhesive is made tacky by heat and is pressed on to the document under high pressure. After cooling, the adhesive **solidifies** and provides a **permanent** bond between the document and laminate film.

Cold laminating is a process in which only one side of a document is laminated. The surface of a document is flooded with a water-soluble adhesive. It is then sent through a set of rollers with the laminating film rolled on to the top of the document and the adhesive. Pressure is applied, which evenly distributes the adhesive and bonds the film to the document. The adhesive takes longer to dry, or cure, than in thermal laminating.

Figure 2.23 Thermal laminating

Varnishing

Varnishing is a general term used to describe a process where a liquid coat is applied to a printed surface. Varnishing a printed document will:

- produce a gloss or matt finish
- increase colour absorption
- speed up the drying process
- 'lock in' the ink under a protective coat, preventing the ink rubbing off.

Varnish can be applied as a spot covering, to emphasise a particular image on the sheet, or as an overall (flood) coating. Varnish is really ink without pigment (or colour). It can be wet-trapped (printed in-line at the same time as other inks) or dry-trapped (run as an additional pass through the press after the initial ink coating has dried). The latter often provides a glossier finish.

UV (ultraviolet) coating, or varnish, is a clear liquid spread over the paper like ink and then cured instantly with ultraviolet light. Since it is cured with light and not heat, no solvents enter the atmosphere.

Aqueous coating is more environmentally friendly than UV coating because it is water based. It does not seep into the paper, and does not crack or scuff easily. Aqueous coatings do, however, cost twice as much as varnish.

Spirit varnish is mixed with a solvent and dries by evaporation of the solvent. Spirit varnish can be harmful to the environment.

Figure 2.24 UV varnishing

Embossing

Embossing is the process of creating a three-dimensional image or design on paper and other sheet material. It is typically achieved with a combination of heat and pressure on the paper. A metal die (female), usually made of brass, and a counter die (male) come together to squeeze the fibres of the material and raise the level of the image.

The embossing process can be used in conjunction with ink – called colour register embossing – or with no ink – called blind embossing. Embossing is usually a separate stage in the production process, after varnishing or laminating.

Figure 2.25 Embossing

Hot foil printing

Hot foil printing is often used to produce gold or silver lettering on cards or invitations. The process requires a 'hot foil' machine that is capable of heating up a plate and applying pressure. The plate is usually made of magnesium or copper. The foil comes on a roll that, when sandwiched between the item being printed and the plate, releases the foil from the roll in the areas that the plate touches.

Hot foil is the only true way of printing glossy gold or silver as ink printing dries matt. Hot foiling can only be printed one colour at a time. It is not capable of full colour, although **holographic** and multi-coloured foils are available.

Figure 2.26 **Hot foil printing**

Die cutting or stamping

Die cutting or stamping is the process of cutting and creasing sheets of material. The die cutters are like 'pastry cutters' mounted in a press, which are then forced down on to the material. The main processes are:

- cutting – separating the material completely
- creasing – making an indentation that will allow thicker material to fold
- hole punching – making a window or opening.

Die cutting is a fast and efficient process, **replicating** the same perfect shape over and over again. Paper, card and sheet plastic can all be die cut.

Figure 2.27 **Commercial die cutting or stamping**

Folding

A paper folding machine will improve accuracy and reduce the time required to fold documents. Some photocopying machines will copy and fold pieces of paper. The two main types of fold are parallel and right angle.

Parallel folds are folds that run alongside one another and do not **intersect**. These are the most popular folds, and are used regularly in businesses because they are easy to read and use. You can use parallel folds to create tri-fold brochures or to fold stationery to be inserted into envelopes.

Right-angle folds run perpendicular (at right angles) to the previous folds on the sheet of paper. This style of fold is more complicated, and is often used for dramatic image presentations, some pop-up books and brochures that unroll in front of the reader.

| Parallel fold | Right-angle fold |

Figure 2.28 Paper folds

Collating

Collating is the process of arranging printed sheets into the desired **sequence**. For example, an eight-page booklet must have all the pages in the correct order, with page 1 at the front and page 8 at the end. Many photocopy machines will copy, fold and collate simple booklets.

Figure 2.29 Photocopying machine

Binding

Binding is the process of holding a printed document together. There are many types of binding but some of the most common are explained below.

Ring binding uses folders with metal or plastic rings that open and close to allow pages to be added or removed easily. Two-ring A4 folders are the most common but other sizes and numbers of rings are available. Ring binding is a good choice for manuals where pages may need to be inserted from time to time. The folders used in ring binding can be printed to include a company name or logo.

Plastic strips slide along the edge of loose pages to hold them together. The strip is 'sprung' apart (with your fingers) to allow it to go over the edge of the sheets. When it is released it closes and grips the sheets. Plastic strips are a cheap and efficient way of holding documents together.

Spiral binding uses either plastic or metal spirals that go through holes in the document. This method allows the finished booklet to open out so that the pages are flat.

Thermal binding is a method of securing loose printed pages with a strip of tape or plastic that has an adhesive applied to it. The document is collated, placed in a machine and the adhesive softened by heat. When the document is removed from the machine the adhesive cools and the pages are held in position.

Saddle-stitching, or saddle stapling, is common for small booklets and calendars, and some magazines. Several sheets of paper are folded (the fold becomes the spine of the booklet) and two or more staples are placed in the fold.

Perfect binding puts all the pages together, roughens and flattens the edge, then a flexible adhesive attaches the paper cover to the spine. Paperback books are a good example of perfect binding. Compared to other binding methods, perfect binding is quite durable and relatively cheap.

Case or edition binding is the most common type of binding for hardback books. It involves sewing the individual sheets together, flattening the spine, and applying end sheets and a strip of cloth to the spine. The hard covers are then attached. The spine of a case-bound hardcover book is usually rounded and there are hinges (grooves) along the edges of the cover near the spine.

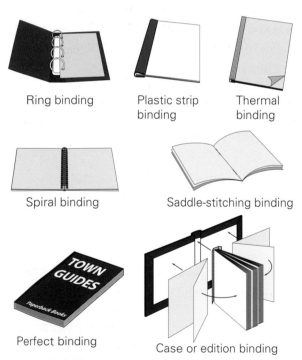

Figure 2.30 Binding methods

KEY POINT

Finishing processes that are applied to graphic materials are usually things that are done to a flat sheet of material after it has been printed. They include such processes as varnishing or binding.

EXAMINER'S TIP

Make sure you can justify the selection of appropriate finishing processes for graphic materials – for example, where and why would you use embossing?

KEY TERMS

AQUEOUS – water based
AUTOMATED – carried out by machines
HOLOGRAPHIC – appears three-dimensional
INTERSECT – to cross over each other
PERMANENT – cannot be removed
REPLICATED – repeated
SEQUENCE – order
SOLIDIFIES – sets
UV – ultraviolet light used to cure UV varnish
SPIRIT – a substance that allows varnish to dry by evaporation

QUESTIONS

1. Name four methods of binding a document.

2. Explain what is meant by the term spot varnishing.

3. Use sketches and notes to show the difference between parallel and right-angle folds.

2.6 SMART AND MODERN MATERIALS

LEARNING OUTCOMES

By the end of this section you should have developed a knowledge and understanding of:

- what is meant by a smart material
- what is meant by a modern material
- common types of smart and modern materials.

Smart materials are called smart because they sense conditions in their environment and respond to those conditions. They appear to 'think' and have a 'memory' as they will revert back to their original state time and time again.

*Modern materials are developed through the invention or creation of new or improved processes. Many modern materials are developed for specialised **applications**, such as space exploration, but some eventually become available for general use.*

Nanotechnology will make a significant contribution to the development of smart and modern materials. An internet search will give you an idea of the latest materials and their applications.

▶ Smart and modern materials

The examples below show some of the common smart and modern materials and their applications.

Thermochromic colours

Thermochromic colours change colour in response to a temperature change. The colours are usually mixed with a **PVA** base medium and painted on to a surface. The colour disappears above a temperature of 27°C and reappears below that temperature. For example, an image painted on to a mug in thermochromic colours will disappear when a hot drink is poured into the mug and reappear once the mug has cooled. Thermochromic colours have many applications in the area of safety products.

Figure 2.31 Mug with a design in thermochromic colours

Photochromic colours

Photochromic colours change colour in response to a change in the level of light. The colours are usually mixed in with a PVA base medium and painted on to a surface. The colour becomes more intense when exposed to bright sunlight. For example, a message printed on to a T-shirt in photochromic colours will appear in the strong sunlight and disappear once the person has moved into the shade. Photochromic colours have many novelty applications.

Figure 2.32 T-shirt with a design in photochromic colours

Phosphorescent pigment

Phosphorescent **pigments** store light energy from natural or artificial light and provide a unique 'afterglow'. The pigment is usually mixed in with a PVA base medium and painted on to a surface. The pigment will then glow in the dark. For example, if the numbers on a watch face are printed in phosphorescent pigment they will be visible at night. Phosphorescent pigments have many applications in the area of safety signs.

Figure 2.33 Door sign with a design in phosphorescent colours

Smart grease

Smart grease is a gel that can be used to 'damp' or slow mechanical systems to provide smooth movement. It will control the release of energy from a wind-up motor, rubber band or spring, and provide a consistent output.

Polymorph

Polymorph is a polymer that can be used for model making and prototyping. It is purchased in **granules** but when heated to just 62°C, usually by placing in water, it fuses together and becomes easily mouldable. It has working properties similar to those of polythene and nylon. Polymorph is a true thermoplastic and can be reused and recycled. It is an ideal material for producing unusual 'one-off' components and parts that cannot be moulded easily.

Figure 2.34 **Polymorph**

Smart wire

Smart wire is an engineered **alloy** that changes length in response to a temperature change. It shrinks in length by about 5% of its original size when a current passing through it provides heat. This in turn provides a useful pulling force that enables it to activate small mechanisms. Once the heating current is removed, a force from a light tension spring or elastic band restores the wire to its original length.

Smart images

Smart images are thin polyester films with embossed holographic-effect metal foils, often giving a three-dimensional effect. These films offer a range of visually interesting and unique optical applications that are increasingly seen on packaging, credit cards and point-of-sale displays.

Figure 2.35 **Holographic foil**

Nanotechnology

Nanotechnology is the science of the extremely small. It involves the study and use of materials on a very small scale. Nano refers to a nanometre (nm). One nanometre is a millionth of a millimetre, or about one-eighty-thousandth the width of a human hair.

One thing that all nanotechnologies have in common is their tiny size. They exploit the fact that, at this scale, materials can behave very differently from when they are in larger form. Nanomaterials can be stronger or lighter, or conduct heat or electricity in a different way. They can even change colour; particles of gold can appear red, blue or gold, depending on their size.

These special attributes are already being used in a number of ways, such as in making computer chips, healthcare products and mobile telephones. Researchers are progressively finding out more about the nanoscale world and aim to use nanotechnologies to create new devices that are faster, lighter, stronger or more efficient.

EXAMINER'S TIP

Test questions will ask you to name different types of smart or modern materials and appropriate applications.

KEY POINT

Smart materials respond to a change in their environment such as a temperature or light change. Modern materials have been developed due to advances in material technology. Nanotechnology will make a significant contribution to the development of smart and modern materials. An internet search will give you a good idea of the latest materials and their applications.

KEY TERMS

ALLOY – mixture of two or more metals
APPLICATION – use
GRANULES – small particles
PIGMENT – a colour
PVA – polyvinyl acetate (a glue commonly used in graphics)

QUESTIONS

1. Write a brief definition of a smart material.

2. Use sketches and notes to explain one use for a thermochromic ink.

3. State what causes a photochromic colour to change its appearance.

2.7 ENVIRONMENTAL AND SUSTAINABILITY ISSUES

LEARNING OUTCOMES

By the end of this section you should have developed a knowledge and understanding of:

• what is meant by an environmental issue

• why products need to be sustainable

• what we can do to make products more environmentally friendly and sustainable.

*Environmental issues are caused by manufacturers producing products that have a harmful effect on the **environment**. For example, during manufacture a product might use chemicals that are dangerous to the environment. Products that have a harmful effect on the environment are not **sustainable**. This means that they will not last because they cannot be allowed to continue to harm the environment. This section is concerned with looking at things that we can do to make the use of materials more environmentally friendly, and hence make products sustainable.*

▶ Environmentally friendly and sustainable use of materials

Selection of materials

The selection of materials will have a major impact on whether a product is environmentally friendly. Materials are either non-renewable (finite) or renewable (infinite).

Non-renewable materials are from substances that have accumulated over millions of years. They cannot be replaced in terms of a human life span. Even though vast reserves of some of these substances exist they will effectively be exhausted in a relatively short period of time. Common non-renewable materials are metals, most plastics and fossil fuels.

Renewable materials can be replaced in a human life span. If grown using methods that are sensitive to the environment these materials will contribute to sustainable development and have a positive environmental benefit. Common renewable materials include wood, wool, jute and straw.

You should always try to use renewable materials when making products.

Figure 2.36 Jute product

Economic use of materials

Economic use of materials means to use only the minimum amount of material required to allow the product to function as intended. This can be achieved by:

- removing parts that are not required for the product to function
- reducing the amount of material used
- rethinking the design concept.

For example, it might be possible to 'remove' a card box that is used to package a bottle of shampoo (is the box really necessary?) or 'reduce' the thickness of foam board used to make a point-of-sale display stand. It might also be possible to 'rethink' the packaging for some products. Do bananas need packaging at all?

Designers and manufacturers have to work hard to convince customers that, in this case, less might be better.

Environmentally friendly manufacture and distribution

An eco footprint is a measure of the resources used by industry or an individual. We all need to reduce our eco footprint in order to be more environmentally friendly.

Figure 2.37 Green initiatives

Manufacturing can be made more environmentally friendly by:

- using energy-efficient factories
- using energy-efficient equipment
- using materials economically to create as little waste as possible
- finding uses for waste material.

Distribution of products can be made more environmentally friendly by:

- reducing the distance products travel
- choosing more fuel-efficient methods of transport.

Many manufacturers are rising to the challenge of behaving in a more environmentally friendly way. An internet search will give you a good idea of some of the 'green' **initiatives** that are being developed.

Design for recycling

In the past designers have mainly been concerned with how products perform during their useful life. Design for recycling means thinking about recycling materials when a product reaches the end of its useful life. Materials will be easier to **recycle** if they:

- can easily be identified
- can easily be separated
- are not contaminated.

You should think very carefully before using materials that cannot easily be recycled. For example, laminated paper is very difficult to recycle because the polyester film cannot easily be separated from the paper.

KEY POINTS

The use of materials can be made more environmentally friendly and sustainable by:

- careful selection of materials
- economic use of materials
- environmentally friendly manufacture and distribution
- designing products so that the materials can easily be recycled.

EXAMINER'S TIP

Test questions may ask you to comment on ways in which designers and manufacturers can make their products more environmentally friendly and sustainable.

KEY TERMS

DISTRIBUTION – to move things around
ENVIRONMENT – concerned with the world in which we live
INITIATIVE – an idea
RECYCLE – to use again
SUSTAINABLE – able to last over time

QUESTIONS

1. Explain what is meant by an environmental issue.
2. Explain what is meant by the term sustainable.
3. Name two non-renewable materials.
4. Name two renewable materials.
5. Explain one way in which manufacturers can make the use of materials more environmentally friendly.

2.8 PRE-MANUFACTURED COMPONENTS

LEARNING OUTCOMES

By the end of this section you should have developed a knowledge and understanding of:

- what is meant by the term pre-manufactured component
- why we use pre-manufactured components
- common types of pre-manufactured component.

A pre-manufactured component is something that is made elsewhere and bought ready for use. For example, you would buy masking tape rather than making it yourself.

▶ Why choose pre-manufactured components?

Standard pre-manufactured components are chosen because:

- it is more **cost-effective** than making the item yourself

- it is not practical to make the item with school-based technology.

For example, you could not hope to make paper clips as cheaply as you can purchase them, and it is not practical to make small electronic components, such as **LEDs**, with school-based technology. The selection of appropriate pre-manufactured components should enhance any project, so don't be afraid to use them wisely.

▌ Types of pre-manufactured component

A wide range of pre-manufactured components is available through suppliers of modelling materials. A brief overview of some types of pre-manufactured component is given below, but an internet search will reveal many more that you can use in your graphics work.

Self-adhesive labels and tapes

Self-adhesive labels come in a wide range of geometrical shapes and can be used to show features on a model, such as windows or doors. Self-adhesive tapes are thin strips of material, on a roll like masking tape, that can be used to mark out areas. Both labels and

Figure 2.38 Self-adhesive labels and tapes

tapes can be pre-printed with numbers, letters or words. Self-adhesive means that the material does not require glue to fasten it to a surface.

Fasteners (fixings or joiners)

Fasteners join materials together in a **temporary** or **permanent** fashion. Good examples of fasteners are paper clips, press-fit click fasteners, eyelets, screws and click rivets. Most of these do not require specialist equipment, other than perhaps a screwdriver, to join the materials, and are relatively cheap to purchase. Care must be taken to select the correct fastener for the material you are using. For example, corriflute fasteners only really work well on corriflute.

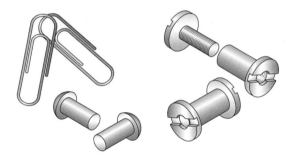

Figure 2.39 Fasteners

Velcro™ is a brand name of fabric 'hook and loop' fasteners. It consists of two layers: a 'hook' side and a 'loop' side. When the two sides are pressed together, the 'hooks' catch in the 'loops' and hold the pieces together. The strips can easily be separated by pulling them apart, making Velcro™ a very good temporary fastener.

Pre-formed and printed sheets

Pre-formed sheets have been formed, often by a process known as vacuum forming, so that the surface is textured to look like stone or brick. Printed sheets are not textured but

Figure 2.40 Pre-formed and printed sheets

have designs printed directly on to the surface. These sheets can be used with good effect to build the walls and roofs of model buildings.

Model components

There are many different types of model component, such as figures that **represent** cars, trees, people, or miniature furniture. Most of these are injection moulded in a thermoplastic. It is very important to choose the correct **scale** (size) parts or your finished model will look out of proportion.

Figure 2.41 Model parts

KEY POINT

A pre-manufactured component is something that is purchased rather than made. Pre-manufactured components are used because it is more cost-effective to do so or because it is very difficult to make the components with school-based technology.

EXAMINER'S TIP

Make sure you can give a definition of a pre-manufactured component, and when it is appropriate to use them.

KEY TERMS

COST-EFFECTIVE – cheaper
LED – light emitting diode
PERMANENT – not removable
REPRESENTS – looks like something
SCALE – drawing or model size relative to actual size
SELF-ADHESIVE – does not require glue to stick to a surface
TEMPORARY – removable

QUESTIONS

1. Explain what is meant by the term pre-manufactured component.
2. Give two reasons why you would use a pre-manufactured component.
3. Name two types of pre-manufactured component.

CHAPTER 3

TOOLS, EQUIPMENT AND PROCESSES

3.1 BASIC GRAPHIC SHAPES

By the end of this section you should have developed a knowledge and understanding of:

- geometrical shapes, and be able to recognise, name and draw a range of them.

Geometrical shapes are used in the design of many products, such as logos, signs and nets (developments) for packaging. These shapes are all 'flat' or, more correctly, two-dimensional (2D).

▶ Triangles

There are four types of **triangle** that you need to know about:

1. right-angle
2. isosceles
3. equilateral
4. scalene.

Drawing a triangle

If you know the length of each side of a triangle, the easiest way to draw it is to use a pair of compasses. Start by drawing one side, AB, as shown in Figure 3.1.

You now need to set your compasses to the length of the second side, AC, and draw an arc from point A.

The compass now needs to be set to the length of the third side, BC, and you draw an arc from B so that the two arcs cross. Complete the triangle by drawing the other two sides.

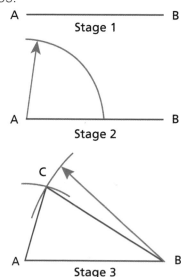

Figure 3.1 Drawing a triangle

Some triangles can be drawn using a protractor to measure the angles, and compasses to mark off the lengths of the sides.

Right-angle triangle

A good example of a right-angle triangle is a set square, as shown in Figure 3.2. It has one angle of 90 degrees – a right angle.

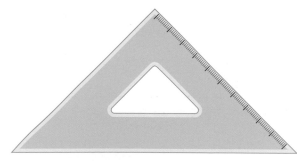

Figure 3.2 A set square

Isosceles triangle

This type of triangle has two sides and two angles the same. For example, the 45-degree set square shown in Figure 3.3 is an isosceles triangle.

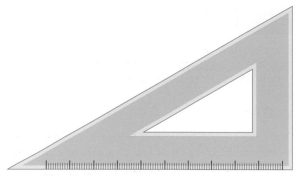

Figure 3.3 A 45-degree set square

Equilateral triangle

The shapes of the road signs shown in Figure 3.4 are in the form of an equilateral triangle.

Figure 3.4 Road signs

The internal angles of this type of triangle are all 60 degrees, as shown in Figure 3.5, and all the sides are the same length. Because the angles are 60 degrees it is easy to draw an equilateral triangle using a 60-degree set square.

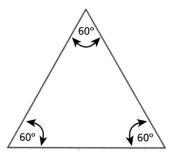

Figure 3.5 Drawing an equilateral triangle

Scalene triangle

The 60/30-degree set square shown in Figure 3.6 is an example of a scalene triangle. None of the angles or sides is the same.

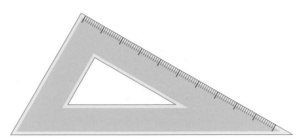

Figure 3.6 A 60/30-degree set square

▶ Quadrilaterals

Shapes that have four straight sides are called **quadrilaterals**. There are four types of quadrilateral that you will need to know about:

1. rectangle
2. square
3. rhombus
4. parallelogram.

Rectangle

Many information signs, like the one shown in Figure 3.7, are rectangular in shape.

Figure 3.7 Information sign

All the corner angles are 90 degrees, and the opposite sides are the same length as shown in Figure 3.8.

To draw an accurate **rectangle** it is best to use a T-square or parallel motion and the 90-degree angle on a set square.

Oblong is another name that is sometimes given to a rectangle.

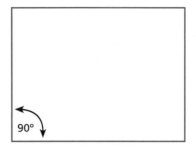

Figure 3.8 Drawing a rectangle

Square

As with a rectangle, all the corner angles are 90 degrees, but the sides of a **square** are all the same length, as shown in Figure 3.9.

A square can be drawn in the same way as a rectangle.

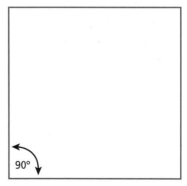

Figure 3.9 Drawing a square

Rhombus

One way of remembering what a **rhombus** looks like is to think of it as a 'squashed square', as shown in Figure 3.10. Like a square, all the sides are the same length and the opposite sides are **parallel**, but it has been 'pushed sideways'.

An accurate rhombus can be drawn using a protractor or set square to measure the angles and a T-square to draw the horizontal lines.

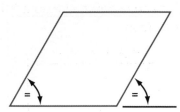

Figure 3.10 Drawing a rhombus

Parallelogram

If a rhombus is a 'squashed square' then a **parallelogram** is a 'squashed rectangle', as shown in Figure 3.11. As with a rectangle, the opposite sides are the same length and are parallel, but the shape has been 'pushed sideways'.

A parallelogram can be drawn in the same way as a rhombus.

Figure 3.11 Drawing a parallelogram

◗ Polygons

A shape that has five or more straight sides is called a **polygon**.

While there are many different types of polygon there are three that you will need to know about:

1. pentagon
2. hexagon
3. octagon.

Pentagon

A **pentagon** has five sides and in some ways is the hardest of the three polygons to draw because you need to accurately measure angles using a protractor.

If you know the length of one side or the size of a circle that the pentagon will fit into you can use compasses and a protractor to draw the shape. To work out the angle to measure you need to divide 360 degrees by 5 (the number of sides); this equals 72 degrees.

If you know how long one side is, measure the first side, AB, and then follow the sequence of lines given in Figure 3.12.

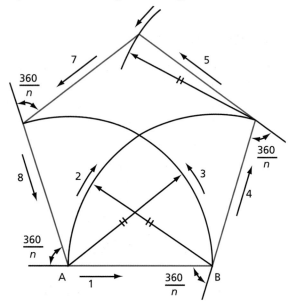

Figure 3.12 Drawing a pentagon

If you want to draw a pentagon in a circle then measure divisions of 72 degrees from the centre, as shown in Figure 3.13, and join up the points around the circumference of the circle.

It is possible to use both these methods to draw any polygon. You just need to work out what angle to use by dividing 360 degrees by

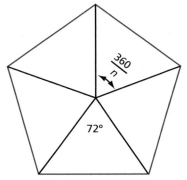

Figure 3.13 Drawing a pentagon in a circle

the number of sides the polygon has. For example, for an octagon, this would be 360 divided by 8, giving you an angle of 45 degrees.

Hexagon

A **hexagon** has six sides.

If you know the length of one of the sides of a hexagon draw a circle whose radius is the length of one side. You can then mark off the radius around the circle and join up the points as shown in Figure 3.14.

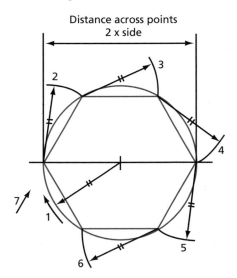

Figure 3.14 Drawing a hexagon in a circle

You can also draw a hexagon if you know the distance from one flat side across to the opposite flat side. This is called the 'distance across the flats', or A/F for short.

Using a T-square or parallel motion and a 30-degree set square you can follow the sequence of lines shown in Figure 3.15 to draw the hexagon.

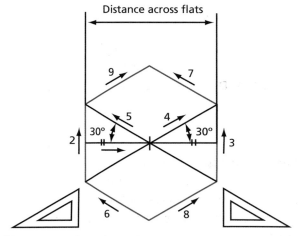

Figure 3.15 Drawing a hexagon

Octagon

An **octagon** has eight sides.

If you know the length of the sides of an octagon, start by drawing one side, AB, and then follow the sequence of lines shown in Figure 3.16 to complete the shape. You can

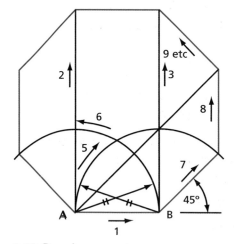

Figure 3.16 Drawing an octagon

use either a protractor or a set square to measure the 45-degree angles.

As with the hexagon, you can sometimes be told the distance across the flats of an octagon. Start by drawing a square, one side of which is the same as the distance across the flats (A/F). Place the point of a pair of compasses on one corner of the square, open the compasses to the centre of the square and draw an arc. Repeat this from each corner, as shown in Figure 3.17, and join up the points to produce the complete octagon.

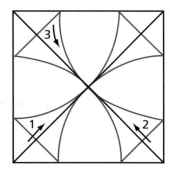

Figure 3.17 Drawing an octagon in a square

Ellipse

Some **ellipses** can be drawn using templates, but these are not always available in the sizes that you might need.

In order to draw an ellipse there are two sizes you need to know. These are the major axis, M, and the minor axis, m, as shown in Figure 3.18.

Although there are several different methods that you could use to draw an ellipse you only need to know about one of them.

The two most common methods are explained here.

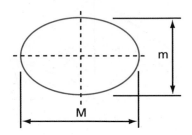

Figure 3.18 Major and minor axes

The trammel method

This uses a strip of paper or card with two distances marked on it, as shown in Figure 3.19. Point A stays on the minor axis, point B stays on the major axis and a dot is marked on the paper at C giving you a point on the ellipse. The trammel is moved and another dot marked. This process is repeated until there are sufficient dots that can be joined to produce the ellipse. The more dots you mark, the better the final curve will be.

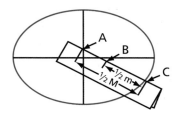

Figure 3.19 Drawing an ellipse using a trammel

The concentric circle method

You start this method by drawing two circles with the same centre (concentric circles). The diameter of the larger circle is the same as the major axis and the diameter of the smaller one the same as the minor axis. The sequence of lines required to complete the drawing of the ellipse is shown in Figure 3.20.

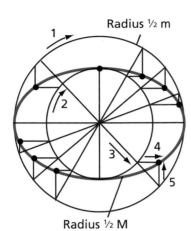

Radius ½ m

Radius ½ M

Figure 3.20 Concentric circle method of drawing an ellipse

Both methods produce a series of points that have to be joined up to produce the final ellipse. This can be done freehand or with the help of drawing aids such as a flexi curve or French curves.

EXAMINER'S TIP

One way of helping you to remember the names of different shapes and how to draw them is to think of a logo or sign that uses that shape. For example, the background of the Boots logo is an ellipse, and many road signs are triangular.

ACTIVITY

1. Collect examples of logos that use geometrical shapes, stick them on a sheet of A3 paper and see how many of the shapes you can name and draw. This will act as a good revision sheet.

2. There is a special relationship between equilateral triangles and hexagons. Use a drawing and notes to explain how they are 'related'.

3. The particular shape of a road sign (circle, triangle, etc.) has a meaning.
   (a) Collect examples of the different shapes that are used.
   (b) Find out the meaning of each different shape.
   (c) Why do you think different shapes are used?

KEY TERMS

ELLIPSE – like a 'flattened' circle; it has one long (major, M) axis and one shorter (minor, m) axis
HEXAGON – a six-sided shape
OCTAGON – an eight-sided shape
PARALLEL – lines that are always the same distance apart
PARALLELOGRAM – looks like a 'squashed rectangle'; opposite sides are parallel and the same length

PENTAGON – a five-sided shape
POLYGON – any shape with five or more sides
QUADRILATERAL – any four-sided shape
RECTANGLE – corners are 90 degrees, opposite sides are parallel and the same length
RHOMBUS – looks like a 'squashed square'; all sides are the same length, opposite sides are parallel
SQUARE – has four sides of the same length
TRIANGLE – three-sided shape; the four types of triangle are right-angle, isosceles, equilateral and scalene

3.2 DRAWING SYSTEMS

LEARNING OUTCOMES

By the end of this section you should have developed a knowledge and understanding of:

- third-angle orthographic projection
- isometric drawing
- planometric drawing
- one-point perspective
- two-point perspective
- assembly drawings
- exploded views
- pictograms.

Being able to use and understand drawing systems will help you to both gather and communicate information and ideas.

These systems use a common 'drawing language' that all designers and manufacturers can understand and use.

Third-angle orthographic projection

Third-angle orthographic projection combines a number of 2D drawings to give details about a 3D object. There could be just a single view or as many as six separate views of an object. However, the three views most commonly used are called the plan, the front view and the end view.

This type of drawing is useful when accurate details about the shape and size of an object need to be communicated.

The **plan** view looks directly down on the top of the object. You may hear this called a 'bird's eye view' but that is not its correct name.

The view of the object that shows the most detail about the object usually becomes the **front view**. This is drawn below the plan view.

The view looking at the left side of the object is drawn to the left of the front view and the view looking at the right side of the object is drawn to the right of the front view. These are called end views.

All the views must be in line with each other, as illustrated in the **orthographic drawing** of a perfume bottle shown in Figure 3.21.

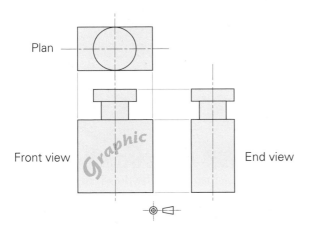

Figure 3.21 Third-angle orthographic drawing of a perfume bottle

Feint construction lines are projected from one view to another to make sure that details are in the correct place and are the correct size.

The symbol shown at the bottom of Figure 3.21 indicates that it is a third-angle orthographic drawing.

Square grids

Orthographic drawings such as the one shown in Figure 3.21 can be produced on plain paper using drawing instruments such as a T-square or parallel motion and a set square, or on squared paper, as shown in Figure 3.22.

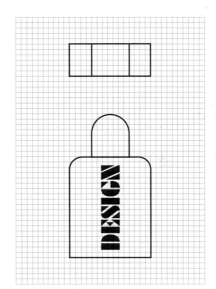

Figure 3.22 Using square grids

Square grid paper is available with different-size squares – for example, 2 mm, 5 mm and 10 mm. It can help you to produce orthographic sketches and drawings quickly because the drawings can be done without a lot of measuring – you just count the number of squares. Accurate drawings can frequently be produced using only a minimal amount of drawing equipment.

 EXAMINER'S TIP

Practise using square grids to produce accurate drawings. You will need to use this technique in the examination.

Hidden detail

Hidden detail lines are drawn as a series of thin, short dashes, like this:

— — — — — — — — — — -

They are used to show parts of an object that cannot directly be seen, such as the internal detail of the mug shown in Figure 3.23.

Figure 3.23 Using hidden detail

Scale drawings

Wherever possible, it is best to draw objects full size. For example, the stamp shown in Figure 3.24 has been drawn full size; this is called a scale of 1:1.

Figure 3.24 Full-size drawing of a stamp

However, some of the detail on the stamp is hard to see and would be clearer if the drawing was larger. Figure 3.25 shows the stamp enlarged to twice its original size – a scale of 2:1 – and, as you can see, the detail is easier to see.

Recommended enlargement scales are 2:1, 5:1, 10:1 and 20:1.

Figure 3.25 Enlarged view of stamp

Plans of buildings and maps like the one shown in Figure 3.26 are examples of things that would need to be drawn smaller than their actual size.

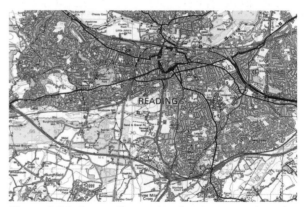

Figure 3.26 A map has to be drawn to a reduced scale

Recommended reduction scales are 1:2, 1:5, 1:10, 1:20, 1:50 and 1:100.

For example, an object drawn to a scale of 1:2 is drawn half its actual size.

Dimensioning

Measurements need to be added to working drawings so that the product can be made to the correct size even when the drawings are the wrong size.

In order that the **dimensions** you add to a

drawing can easily be read and understood you need to:

- make sure that all the measurements can be read from the bottom right-hand corner of the paper
- draw limit lines out from the object and write the sizes above a dimension line, with arrows at each end, that stretches between the limit lines
- place smaller measurements closer to the drawing
- make sure that all measurements refer to the actual size of the object (remember, this will not always be the same size as the drawing you have produced); sizes should be in millimetres (mm), but it is not necessary to write 'mm' on the drawing.

Look at how the dimensions have been correctly added to the drawing of the mug shown in Figure 3.27.

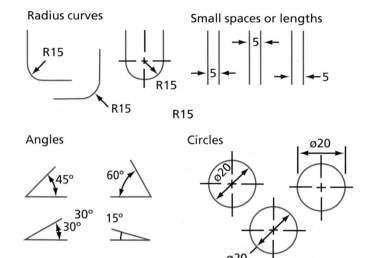

Figure 3.28 Correct dimensioning methods

EXAMINER'S TIP

Always use millimetres (mm) to dimension your drawing; you only need to write the number.

Sectional views

A good way of showing the internal detail or structure of an object is to draw a **cut-away (sectional) view**.

For example by cutting through the chocolate bars shown in Figure 3.29 the ingredients can clearly be seen.

When drawing a sectional view you should:

- draw parallel lines at an angle of 45 degrees across the cut surface; this is called **cross-hatching**
- cross-hatch different parts in different directions or at a different angle; in addition, colour can also be used to emphasise the cut surfaces
- show where the section has been taken and label the sectional view.

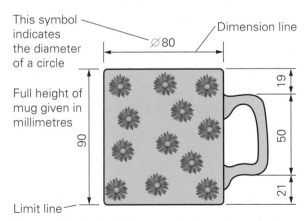

Figure 3.27 Adding dimensions to a drawing

Figure 3.28 shows how to correctly dimension features such as circles, the radius of curves, small sizes and angles.

Figure 3.30 shows how to correctly lay out and label a drawing that includes a sectional view.

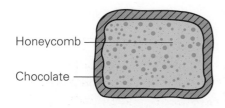

Honeycomb

Chocolate

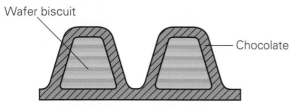

Wafer biscuit

Chocolate

Figure 3.29 Sectional views of chocolate bars

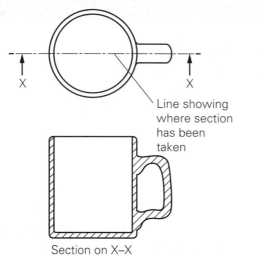

X   X

Line showing where section has been taken

Section on X–X

Figure 3.30 Producing a drawing that includes a sectional view

KEY POINTS

- Orthographic drawings are a good way of presenting working drawings. They can contain all the information required to make a product.
- Sectional views can be included when you want to give more detail about the 'inside' of the product.

EXAMINER'S TIPS

- If you are drawing a sectional view, always cross-hatch areas that have been cut through.
- Make sure you know the names of the different views and how they should be laid out.
- Check the level of detail required in a question. For example, how many views do you need to draw; do you need to include hidden detail; what scale have you got to use; are dimensions required?
- Make sure you plan your answer so that what you need to draw will fit into the space you have available.

KEY TERMS

CROSS-HATCHING – close parallel lines at 45 degrees, used to show a cut surface on a sectional view
CROSS-SECTION – the cut face showing when you cut through an object
CUT-AWAY (SECTIONAL) VIEW – a drawing that shows part of the object removed to reveal the inside
DIMENSION – to add measurements (sizes) to a drawing
FRONT VIEW – two-dimensional (2D) view that usually gives you the most detail about an object
HIDDEN DETAIL – dashed (dotted) lines used to indicate parts of an object that cannot directly be seen
ORTHOGRAPHIC DRAWING – this shows several views from different positions; it

gives accurate information about the size, shape and proportions of an object

PLAN – two-dimensional (2D) drawing of the top of an object

SQUARE GRID – a framework of guidelines crossing at 90 degrees, used to produce quick, accurate drawings

THIRD-ANGLE ORTHOGRAPHIC – system of drawing where the left-hand end view is shown to the left of the front view, above which is the plan

ACTIVITY

Make an orthographic drawing of a carton of fruit juice. Include the maker's name and all other surface detail.

3.3 THREE-DIMENSIONAL DRAWING METHODS

LEARNING OUTCOMES

By the end of this section you should have developed a knowledge and understanding of four types of three-dimensional drawing:

- isometric
- planometric
- one-point perspective
- two-point perspective.

*By using **three-dimensional (3D) drawings** you will be able to communicate clearly what an object looks like because this type of drawing shows three sides of an object in a single view. 3D drawings are sometimes called pictorial drawings because they are like a 'picture' of an object.*

Isometric drawing

In **isometric** drawing, vertical lines remain vertical and horizontal lines are drawn at 30 degrees. The main items of drawing

equipment that you will need are therefore a T-square and a 30/60-degree set square.

You start most isometric drawings by producing a box into which the object you want to illustrate will fit. This process is sometimes called '**crating**'.

Figure 3.31 shows the stages involved in drawing a box. You start with the corner nearest to you, measure the height, width and length of the object and then draw the rest of the vertical and 30-degree lines required to complete the box.

Once you have the basic box shape, you can

then add and cut away parts to achieve the shape you require.

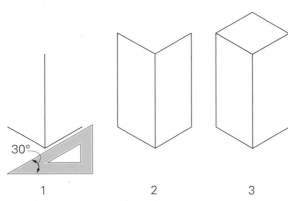

Figure 3.31 Stages in making an isometric drawing

Isometric grids

The grid on isometric paper is in 5 mm sections. You can count the grid sections to get the right sizes, and follow the grid lines to get the right angles, as shown in Figure 3.32.

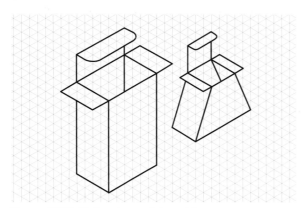

Figure 3.32 Using isometric grids

This enables isometric drawings and sketches to be produced quickly and with a reasonable degree of accuracy.

The **isometric grid** paper can be used under plain paper so that drawings can either be traced through or drawn directly on to the plain paper with the aid of the grid.

Drawing sloping surfaces and lines on an isometric view

Many objects – such as those shown in Figure 3.33 – have sloping surfaces and lines.

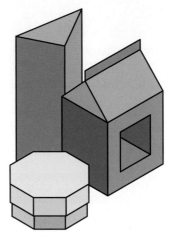

Figure 3.33 Objects with sloping surfaces

To draw a sloping line on an isometric view you need to work out where each end of the line would be and then join the points as shown in Figure 3.34.

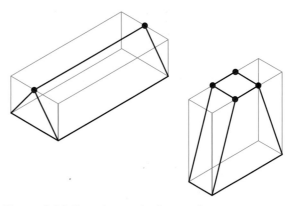

Figure 3.34 Drawing a sloping surface

Drawing circles on an isometric view

All circles on an isometric view appear as ellipses.

The best way to draw these ellipses is to use an isometric **ellipse template**.

The process of using this type of template is shown in Figure 3.35.

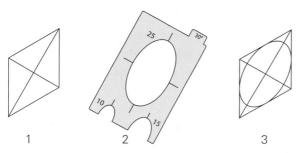

Figure 3.35 Using an isometric ellipse template

- *Stage 1:* draw an isometric square; the side of the square should be the same size as the diameter of the circle.
- *Stage 2:* draw the diagonals on the square, then select the correct size of ellipse and line up the marks on the template with the diagonal lines.
- *Stage 3:* draw round the inside of the template to produce the required ellipse.

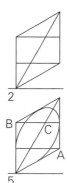
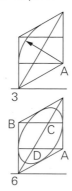
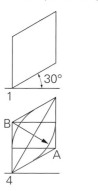

Figure 3.36 Drawing an isometric circle

Figure 3.36 shows, stage by stage, how you can use a pair of compasses to draw four arcs that join to produce an isometric circle. This method is particularly useful for larger sizes where a template may not be readily available.

 EXAMINER'S TIP

Practise using an isometric grid to produce accurate three-dimensional drawings. Make sure that you know how to draw sloping surfaces and circles on an isometric view. You will need all these techniques to answer some of the examination questions.

 KEY POINTS

- Lines that are vertical on the object will be vertical in the drawing.
- Lines that are horizontal on the object will be at 30 degrees on the drawing.
- All measurements on these lines are actual size.
- Circles appear as ellipses on an isometric view.

ACTIVITY

(a) Find some examples of point-of-sale display stands that have been used to advertise a recently released DVD or CD. (A local shop might give you some actual examples or allow you to take some photographs, or you could look on the internet.)

(b) Select an example that you like and produce an isometric drawing or sketch of it. Try to include as much detail as you can, and add colour to your finished piece of work. Perhaps a display could be made of your class's work, along with examples of the display stands and images that you worked from.

KEY TERMS

CRATING – the process of starting an isometric drawing by drawing a box into which the object will just fit

ELLIPSE TEMPLATE – a thin sheet of plastic with ellipses of various sizes cut out so that they can be drawn round

ISOMETRIC – a three-dimensional (3D) drawing method in which most lines are drawn vertically or at 30 degrees

ISOMETRIC GRID – grid with vertical lines and 30-degree lines

THREE-DIMENSIONAL (3D) DRAWING – a drawing that shows the height, length and depth of an object

Exploded views

While 2D and 3D exploded views can be drawn using any appropriate drawing system, isometric views are the ones that you need to be most familiar with and will use the most.

An exploded view is used when you want to show how the separate parts of an object fit together and relate to one another.

When drawing an exploded view it is important that the separate parts line up, that they are in the same order in which they fit together and each part of the object can clearly be seen.

It is a good idea to arrange the parts so that they overlap each other slightly, as shown in Figure 3.37.

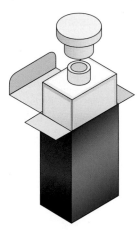

Figure 3.37 Exploded view of perfume bottle and packaging

This gives the drawing a feeling of depth, and it also helps to show how the parts relate to one another and how they fit together.

Planometric drawing

Planometric views are drawn using a T-square or parallel motion and a 45-degree set square.

As with isometric drawing, the best way to start most planometric drawings is to draw a box into which the object you want to draw will just fit.

Figure 3.38 shows how you should start by drawing a true plan of the box rotated round at an angle of 45 degrees.

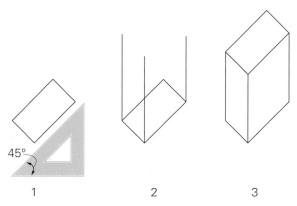

Figure 3.38 Stages in making a planometric drawing

Next, draw vertical lines from the corners of the plan and on one of them measure the height of the box. Complete the top of the box using a 45-degree set square.

Figure 3.39 Planometric drawing of a nail varnish bottle

Any details you add to the top of the box are drawn as true shapes but shapes become distorted when you draw them on the sides.

Because planometric views are projected from true plan views it is very easy to draw cylindrical objects and those like the bottle shown in Figure 3.39, where the plan view involves circles or part circles.

To draw a cylinder you start by drawing a circle, as shown in Figure 3.40. From the centre of the circle draw a vertical line and measure the height of the cylinder. Draw a second circle and finally draw the lines joining the two cylinders to complete the planometric view.

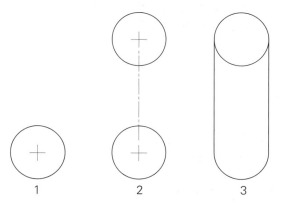

Figure 3.40 Planometric drawing of a cylinder

KEY POINTS

- The true plan of the object is drawn at an angle of 45 degrees to the horizontal.
- Vertical lines are projected up from the plan.
- Circles in the plan view or projected from the plan view remain as true circles.

ACTIVITY

(a) Do an internet search and collect some pictures of famous tall buildings like the Empire State Building in New York, and the BT Tower and Tower 42 in London.

(b) Make a series of sketches that simplify the design of one of the buildings into a number of basic shapes.

(c) Based on your simplified sketches produce a planometric view of the building.

Perspective drawing

The most realistic three-dimensional drawings are produced using **perspective** drawing techniques. You have probably noticed that the further away something is from you the smaller it appears to be. For example, the parallel sides of a long, straight road appear to meet in the distance, as shown in Figure 3.41. This point becomes the **vanishing point** (VP) on a perspective drawing.

Perspective drawing creates the illusion of objects getting smaller and parallel lines getting closer together the further away from us they are. Because perspective drawings are similar to the way we actually see things they can appear very lifelike and are easily understood by most people.

You will need to understand and produce two types of perspective drawing:

1. one-point perspective
2. two-point perspective.

One-point perspective drawing

One point is the simplest form of perspective to draw and is based on a 'flat' view of an object. Lines are then drawn from the various corners of this 'flat' view back to a vanishing point (VP), as shown in Figure 3.42. Depth is then added by drawing lines parallel to the 'flat' view. You cannot easily measure the depth – it has to be estimated.

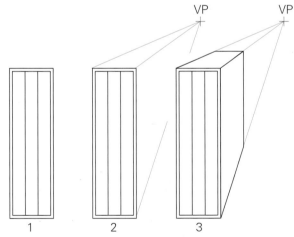

Figure 3.42 Stages in making a one-point perspective drawing of a boxed set of DVDs

Figure 3.41 The vanishing point

ACTIVITY

(a) Copy, to a larger size, the perspective drawing of a boxed set of DVDs shown in Figure 3.42.

(b) Select an appropriate 'theme' for the box set and collect some information about it. Add lettering, graphic images and colour to your drawing, based on your chosen theme.

Figure 3.43 shows you how, by positioning the vanishing point in different positions related to the 'flat' view, it is possible to view an object from the left, from above, from below, from the front or from the right.

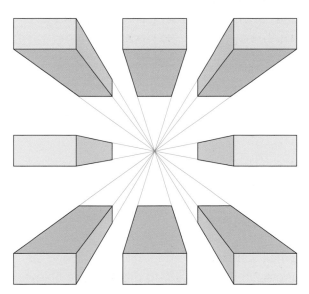

Figure 3.43 Positioning the vanishing point

Using these simple techniques it will not be long before you can draw quite complex one-point perspective drawings such as the one of the kitchen shown in Figure 3.44. This has been viewed from directly above, with the vanishing point positioned in the centre of the floor.

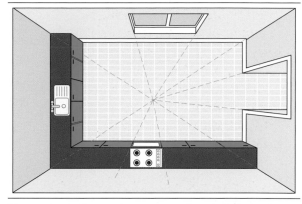

Figure 3.44 One-point perspective drawing of a kitchen

EXAMINER'S TIP

Once you have drawn the basic layout of a room make several photocopies so that you can try different colour schemes.

Two-point perspective drawing

On a two-point perspective drawing the vertical lines remain as vertical lines. The other lines go back to two vanishing points: one to the right and one to the left of the object. These points lie on a horizontal line, which is at eye level.

Choosing the position of the object in relation to eye level enables you to view the object from various heights, as shown in Figure 3.45.

You need to keep the vanishing points as far apart as possible and arrange the drawing so that neither the top nor the bottom of the object is close to the eye-level line. One exception to this is when you are drawing a tall building and want to give the impression of

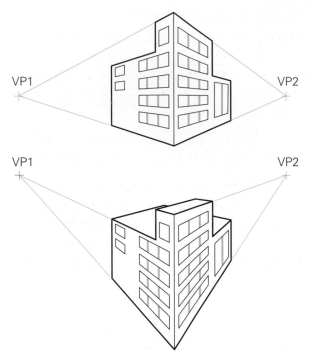

Figure 3.45 Viewing an object from different heights

looking up at it. In this situation you would position both vanishing points in line with the bottom of the building, as shown in Figure 3.46.

As with the other types of three-dimensional drawing system, it is best to start by drawing a box (or crate) that the object will just fit into.

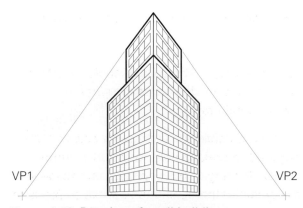

Figure 3.46 Drawing of a tall building

The first step is to draw the corner nearest to you, as shown in Figure 3.47. Then you need to select two vanishing points (VP1 and VP2) and draw lines back to both of them. Next, you need to estimate the length and width required and draw two vertical lines. By connecting the remaining corners of the box to the vanishing point you complete the drawing of the box.

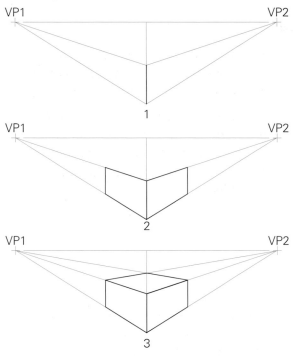

Figure 3.47 Stages in making a two-point perspective drawing

Detail can then be added to the drawing, as shown in Figure 3.48, to produce the object that you set out to draw, in this case a puzzle cube.

VP1   VP2

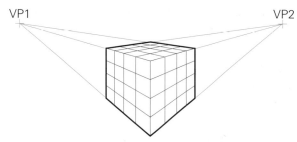

Figure 3.48 Perspective drawing of a puzzle cube

KEY POINTS

- You need to use three-dimensional drawing systems when you want to give a realistic impression of an object
- In a one-point perspective illustration the front surface of the object is drawn 'flat' on the page. Depth is added by projecting lines back to a vanishing point.

KEY TERMS

PERSPECTIVE – how our eyes naturally see things; the further away objects are, the smaller they appear to get
TWO-DIMENSIONAL (2D) DRAWING – a drawing that has length and height
VANISHING POINT – the point where converging lines meet

ACTIVITY

Make two perspective drawings of a cereal box from different viewing positions. Make one box look realistic and the other as big as a house.

Assembly drawings

Many products are made from more than one part. These separate parts (or components, as they are sometimes called) need to be put together in the correct way in order to produce the final product.

A drawing that shows all the parts correctly put together is called an **assembly drawing**.

You could be given, or need to give, details about the parts to be assembled in the form of a three-dimensional **exploded view**, as shown in Figure 3.49, or as a series of orthographic views, as shown in Figure 3.50.

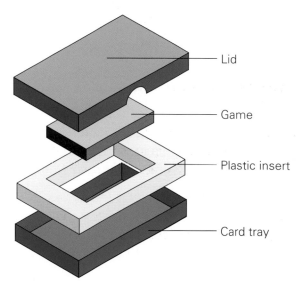

Lid

Game

Plastic insert

Card tray

Figure 3.49 Exploded view of packaging for a video game

The assembly drawing itself could be either an orthographic drawing or a three-dimensional drawing.

Figure 3.50 shows the separate parts required to make a card model of a Jumbo Jet. By looking at the drawings and following the given instructions it is possible to produce the assembly drawing shown in Figure 3.51.

1. Cut out the pieces.
2. Glue together both sides of the fuselage wings and tailplane.
3. Cut out the slots for the wing and tailplane.
4. Curve each engine into a cylinder and glue along the shaded area.
5. Slot in the wing and tailplane and attach the engines with glue in the positions indicated.

Engines

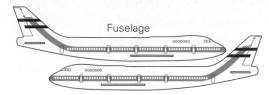

Fuselage

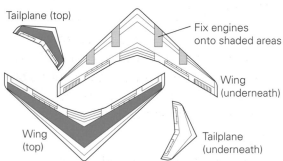

Tailplane (top)

Fix engines onto shaded areas

Wing (underneath)

Wing (top)

Tailplane (underneath)

Figure 3.50 Orthographic views of the parts required to make a model plane

With this example it is reasonably obvious how the parts fit together because written instructions are given.

When faced with less information, however, you need to look for sizes and shapes that will enable one part to fit into or onto another.

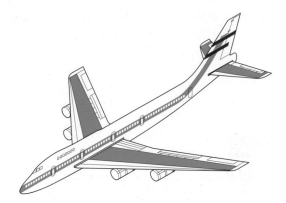

Figure 3.51 Assembly drawing of a model jet

Parts list

This is a table that contains details about all the components that have to be assembled to make a product. It tells you what size the parts are, what they are made from, and so on. You can make your own style of table but it should contain information in a form that is easy to find and follow.

An example of a **parts list** is shown in Figure 3.52.

Assembly instructions

Sometimes you need to provide step-by-step instructions on how to **assemble** a product. The instructions need to be clear and well thought out so that they are easy to understand and follow.

Part	Number required	Material	Length	Width	Thickness
Fuselage (right)					
Fuselage (left)		Card			
Tailplane (top)	1				
Tailplane (underneath)					1000 microns
Engines	4				
Wing (top)					
Wing (underneath)					

Figure 3.52 Parts list

As well as written instructions, drawings can also be used as shown in Figure 3.53.

1. Colour the whale.
2. Using a pair of scissors cut along all of the solid lines. Get an adult to cut out the money slot using a craft knife.
3. Score the dotted lines and carefully fold over all the glue tabs.
4. Glue your whale together as shown in the diagram.

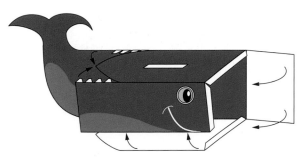

Figure 3.53 Assembly instructions

KEY POINTS

- Exploded drawings are an excellent way of producing instructions and/or constructional details
- Assembly drawings can give details about how the parts of an object fit together and what the assembled object looks like.

KEY TERMS

ASSEMBLE – put together
ASSEMBLY DRAWING – a drawing that shows the separate parts of an object joined together
EXPLODED VIEW – each part of an object is drawn separately but in a way that shows how the parts fit together
PARTS LIST – a table that gives details – such as size, material, etc. – about each of the individual pieces that need to be made and assembled to produce a product

ACTIVITY

(a) Design a simple card model like the jet shown in Figures 3.50 and 3.51.
(b) Using both exploded views and assembly drawings, produce an instruction sheet that explains how to make the model.

▶ Pictograms

Pictograms use stylised pictures and **symbols** to communicate information in a simple and bold way. As pictograms do not generally use words they can be quickly understood regardless of what language people can read.

Pictograms are usually based on the simplified silhouette (outline) of an object. A single bold colour is then added to the silhouette to make it stand out, as shown in Figure 3.54.

Figure 3.54 Examples of pictograms

This means that the pictogram can be seen from a long distance.

Sometimes it is the background that is coloured rather than the silhouette.

Pictograms such as those shown in Figure 3.55 are frequently used at airports, shopping centres, railway and bus stations, and other public places.

Figure 3.55 Pictograms used in public places

Secondary packaging that is transported from one country to another often has pictograms like those shown in Figure 3.56 printed on it. This informs the people handling and moving the packaging about such things as the contents and the type of conditions that it should be kept in.

Figure 3.56 Pictograms used on packaging

When producing your own designs you need to look at existing pictograms and analyse how effective they are. What makes them easy or hard to understand?

A good pictogram is one that is simple, clear, and easy to understand and remember.

KEY TERMS

PICTOGRAM – simple, bold image that is used to communicate information without the use of words

SYMBOL – a letter, figure or drawn sign that represents or identifies an object, process or activity

3.4 ENHANCEMENT TECHNIQUES

LEARNING OUTCOMES

By the end of this section you should have developed a knowledge and understanding of:

- tonal shading
- shadows
- thick and thin line technique
- rendering a drawing using texture.

By using various enhancement techniques on a drawing it is possible to suggest the form (shape) of an object and the material that it is made from.

Tone

If an object is put close to a light source, such as a window, the side facing the window will appear much lighter than the side facing away from the window. These lighter and darker versions of the same colour are called **tones**.

By applying different tones to a drawing you can make the object look more solid, or three-dimensional.

In the drawing of the cube shown in Figure 3.57 you can see three sides of the cube. Each side will reflect a different amount of light and is therefore shaded a different tone.

The general rule that you use when adding tone is to make the sides darker as they turn away from the light, as shown in Figure 3.58.

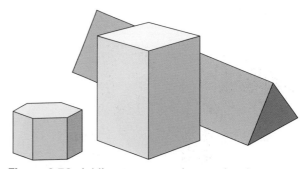

Figure 3.58 Adding tone to enhance the three-dimensional appearance of various shapes

Shading, lines and dots

Figure 3.59 shows how **shading**, lines and dots can be used to achieve variations (or graduations) in tone. The harder you press with an HB pencil, the darker the tone becomes. The closer together you draw the lines or the dots the darker the tone will appear to be.

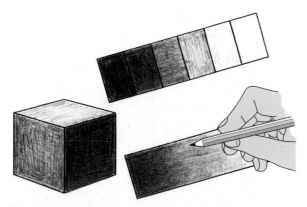

Figure 3.57 Adding tone to a cube

Figure 3.59 Adding tone using shading, lines and dots

Curved surfaces

On curved surfaces, such as the cylinder, cone and sphere shown in Figure 3.60, the amount of light reflected gets less as the surface turns away from the light source and therefore the tone you use needs to get darker. A **highlight** should be included. This is a light, almost white, area that is closest to the light source.

Figure 3.60 Adding tone to curved shapes

▶ Shadows

You can use **shadows** on drawings to increase the feeling of depth and to suggest that the object that you have drawn is resting on a surface rather than 'floating in mid-air'.

The surface can be suggested by drawing a straight line across the paper behind the object, as shown in Figure 3.61. An estimated shadow is good enough to create the effect

that you need for most of your design drawings.

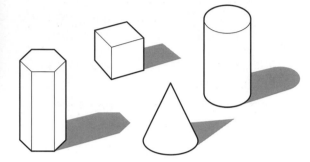

Figure 3.61 Adding a shadow

You need to remember that the shadow will:

- be similar in shape to the object you have drawn, but may be elongated
- be on the side furthest away from the light source
- generally be darker than the darkest tone you have used on the drawing.

▶ Thick and thin lines

Lines are used on a drawing to show the edge where two surfaces meet. You can make the drawing of an object look more three-dimensional and give it impact by using **thick and thin lines**. The thick lines create a

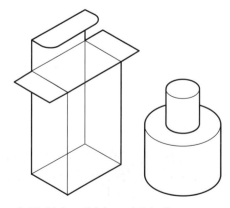

Figure 3.62 Using thick and thin lines

shadow effect, which helps to make the object look more solid, as shown in Figure 3.62.

The following simple rules can help you decide where to use different thicknesses of lines.

- A thick line is used for an edge where only one surface can be seen.
- A thin line is used for an edge where both surfaces can be seen.
- Sometimes, for additional impact, an even thicker line can be drawn around the outline of the drawing.

These rules can be applied to both flat and curved surfaces.

▶ Rendering a drawing using texture

It is important to show **texture** in your design drawings. Not only will it make them look more interesting to look at but it will show the material that you are intending to use in your finished design.

Textural representation uses a combination of shading, lines and dots.

The next part of this section will show you how you can use textural representation to illustrate the following materials.

- wood
- metal (matt and chrome)
- plastic (matt, textured and shiny)
- glass
- concrete.

Wood
Wood can be drawn realistically by looking at the grain patterns, as shown in Figure 3.63.

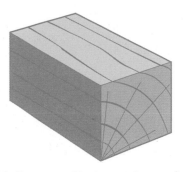

Figure 3.63 Representing a wooden surface

For example, on the end of a natural piece of wood you use a series of curved lines to represent the growth rings. On the side you need to use feint lines that run down the length of the wood. On the third surface the lines need to be more wavy. Do not make any of the lines too bold or dark.

Using a combination of brown, yellow and orange pencil shading can further enhance the drawing.

Matt (dull) metal
A series of straight lines drawn with a ruler, as shown in Figure 3.64, can create a 'hard' effect that is useful for representing metal.

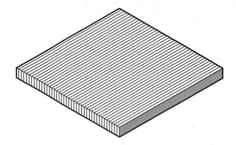

Figure 3.64 Representing a dull metal finish

By altering the distance between the lines, lighter or darker tone is created, which is a good way of representing curved surfaces like the bottle top shown in Figure 3.65.

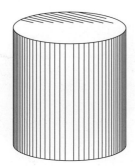

Figure 3.65 Representing curved metal surfaces

Using grey pencil shading can further enhance the drawing.

Chrome and polished metals

On very shiny surfaces, like chrome, reflections will appear as high-contrast areas of dark and light, as shown in Figure 3.66.

Figure 3.66 Representing shiny metal surfaces

Matt plastic

This material can be represented in the same way as matt metal. Once the straight lines have been added, the drawing can be further enhanced by adding pencil shading in an appropriate colour.

Textured plastic

The surface of this type of material is covered in tiny lumps and dents. This texture can be represented by drawing small, irregular shapes over the required area, as shown in Figure 3.67.

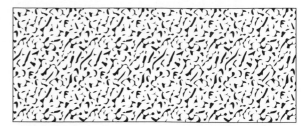

Figure 3.67 Representing textured plastic surfaces

Opaque shiny plastic

It is the highlights and reflections on materials that give them their shiny appearance. The simplest way of suggesting reflection is either to draw a number of short parallel lines across the surface of the object, or to shade the surface evenly with a suitable colour and then rub out wavy lines, as shown in Figure 3.68.

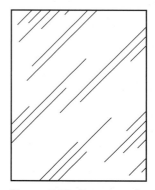

Figure 3.68 Representing surfaces made from opaque shiny plastic

Glass and clear plastic

Because transparent materials have no colour of their own they can be hard to represent. One method that can be very effective is to shade the surface using a light blue pencil and then rub out areas to suggest reflections, as shown in Figure 3.69. Feint broken lines can be used to show details that can be seen through the glass or plastic.

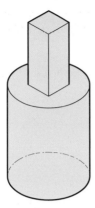

Figure 3.69 Representing transparent materials

Concrete

The surface of concrete is rough. On its surface you can see evidence of sand and ballast (small stones). The sand can be represented by a series of dots while the stones can be suggested by using small irregular shapes, as shown in Figure 3.70.

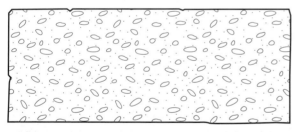

Figure 3.70 Representing concrete surfaces

 EXAMINER'S TIP

Adding texture to your drawings will give them a more realistic appearance. Remember, texture can be added using shading, lines and dots. In an examination situation, add colour and texture to a drawing only when it is specifically asked for in the question.

 KEY TERMS

HIGHLIGHT – a bright area where light is reflected from the edge or surface of an object

RENDERING – applying colour, tone and texture to a drawing

SHADING – a technique used to show how light falls on an object

SHADOW – a dark area formed when an object is in the way of rays of light

TEXTURE – the surface pattern or 'feel' of materials

THICK AND THIN LINES – a drawing technique that uses lines of different thicknesses to make an object look more three-dimensional

TONE – the various shades that can be produced from a single colour

 ACTIVITY

(a) Collect a range of images of products made from different materials. Trace these images on to plain paper to produce line drawings.

(b) Use appropriate rendering techniques on these drawings to produce illustrations that communicate both the form (shape) of the product and the materials that it is made from.

3.5 DATA PRESENTATION

By the end of this section you should have developed a knowledge and understanding of:

- how to translate or transpose written data into a visual form using the following methods:
  - tables
  - line graphs
  - bar charts (2D and 3D)
  - pie charts (2D and 3D)
  - pictographs.

When research such as surveys and questionnaires is carried out, you collect various facts and information. This is known as **data**.

Data is often easier to understand if presented visually rather than in written form or as a series of numbers.

Tables

Tables are useful when you want to make a comparison between two or more items; they are a little bit like a checklist.

For example, the table shown in Figure 3.71 compares the information displayed on packaging for different types of confectionery (sweets).

Information	Bar codes	Product name	Manufacturer	Contact details	List of contents (ingredients)	Best before	Safety warning	Price	Weight or volume
Product									
Packet of mint sweets									
Box of fruit gums									
Chewing gum									
Bar of fruit and nut chocolate									
Bag of mixed sweets									
Bar of organic plain chocolate									

Figure 3.71 Table used to compare information on packaging for sweets

A table can be a good way of both preparing the questions for a survey and recording people's responses. Results are usually recorded by using ticks, crosses, dots or numbers. Ticks, crosses and dots are best used for yes/no-type answers, whereas a 'sliding scale' of numbers, such as 1 to 5, could be used to show varying degrees of liking or not liking something.

You could use a table as a way of checking your design ideas against your specification.

Line graphs

Line graphs are often used to illustrate how something changes over a period of time. For example, the line graph shown in Figure 3.72 plots the position of a CD in the top 20 bestsellers over a four-week period.

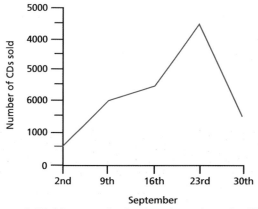

Figure 3.72 Line graph plotting the sales of a CD

If you have more than one line to plot on the same graph, as shown in Figure 3.73, you should use different colours or different types of line.

All line graphs should have a title, and clearly labelled vertical and horizontal axes.

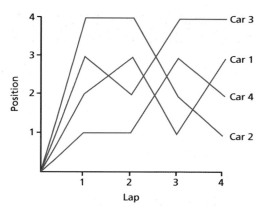

Figure 3.73 Plotting more than one piece of data

Bar charts

A **bar chart** is a simple way of comparing amounts. The amounts can be represented by a series of horizontal or vertical bars (rectangles). The bars are all the same width with a gap between each one. The height (or length) of each bar represents a quantity that can be read off against an appropriate scale, as shown in Figure 3.74. Generally each bar is individually labelled.

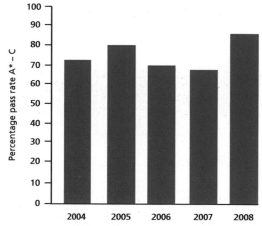

Figure 3.74 Bar chart comparing examination results over a five-year period

Proportional chart

A single bar can be used to produce a proportional chart. The complete bar represents the whole of something. This is then divided up into proportions or percentages, as show in Figure 3.75.

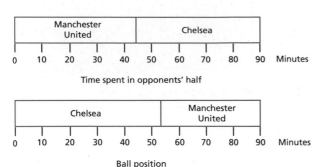

Figure 3.75 Proportional chart illustrating football statistics

Histogram

A **histogram** is very similar to a bar chart but it does not have gaps between the bars, as shown in Figure 3.76.

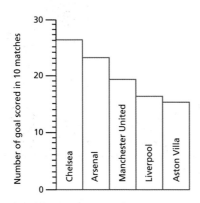

Figure 3.76 Histogram

3D bar charts

You should always try to present graphs and charts in an interesting way. Bar charts can be visually more interesting if you draw them three-dimensionally (3D) rather than two-dimensionally (2D). This will allow you to use a variety of presentation techniques, such as the examples shown in Figure 3.77. The use

of colour and tonal shading can further enhance the presentation.

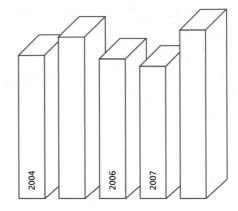

Figure 3.77 Examples of 3D bar charts

Pie charts

A **pie chart** is circular. The circle represents the whole of something, which is then divided into sectors rather like the slices of a cake. Each sector represents a proportion or a percentage of the whole. To produce a pie chart you need to convert numbers or percentages into degrees.

For example, the pie chart shown in Figure 3.78 illustrates the different ways that a class of 30 students travel to school.

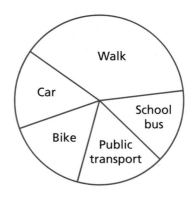

Figure 3.78 Pie chart showing how students travel to school

The circle of the pie chart is made up of 360 degrees, this represents the whole class. The portion of the circle that would represent 1 student would be 360 divided by 30, giving 12 degrees.

You can do a similar calculation for percentages. For example, 40% would be converted as follows: 40 divided by 100 multiplied by 360, giving 144 degrees.

3D pie charts

Greater impact and visual interest can be achieved by making the pie chart three-dimensional, as shown in Figure 3.79. The use of colour and tonal shading can further enhance the presentation of a pie chart.

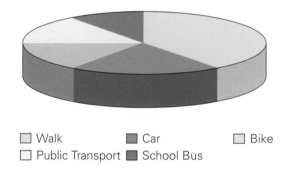

- ☐ Walk
- ☐ Public Transport
- ■ Car
- ■ School Bus
- ☐ Bike

Figure 3.79 Examples of 3D pie charts

Sometimes you might be able to turn the pie chart into a drawing of an appropriate object, such as the cake and coin shown in Figure 3.80.

Isometric is the best form of 3D drawing to use for this type of presentation.

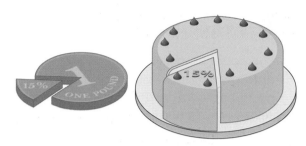

Figure 3.80 Cake and coin pie charts

▶ Pictographs

Simple, stylised pictures or symbols can be used to illustrate the subject of a bar chart. For example, the columns on the histogram shown in Figure 3.76 could be replaced by footballs or football shirts, as shown in Figure 3.81.

Figure 3.81 Pictograph

The symbols used must relate specifically to the subject of the chart and be easy to understand.

This type of chart may need a key to explain the amount that is represented by each symbol.

Pictographs can often be easier to understand than other types of graphs and charts.

EXAMINER'S TIPS

- You could be asked which method of data presentation would be the most appropriate to use in a given situation. Always try to justify your choices.
- You might be asked to produce tables, line graphs, bar charts, pie charts or pictographs to record data given in a question. Alternatively, you might be asked to 'read' information from graphs, charts, etc. that are presented as part of a question.
- Make sure any graphs, charts, etc. that you produce are appropriate to the given situation – do not over-complicate what you are doing. Make sure you focus on what the question is asking you.

KEY TERMS

BAR CHART – uses columns (bars) with spaces between to show how one quantity varies in relation to another

DATA – facts collected for reference

HISTOGRAM – same as a bar chart but with no gaps between the columns

LINE GRAPH – plotted line(s) show how something varies over a period of time

PICTOGRAPH – these are graphs that incorporate symbols or pictograms into their design

PIE CHART – a circular chart which shows something as a percentage or proportion of a whole. The complete circle represents the whole (100%)

TABLE – a list of facts or figures arranged in columns

KEY POINTS

- The information given in tables, graphs and charts must be clear and easy to understand.
- All tables, graphs and charts must be clearly labelled.

ACTIVITY

1. Design a pie chart to show how you spend a typical school day. Think of a day as being 24 hours. How is your day divided up? For example, how many hours do you spend studying, eating, travelling, watching television, on a computer, asleep, etc. Think carefully about how you will give the pie chart interest and impact.

2. Design a table, graph or chart that could be used in a newspaper or magazine to illustrate the result(s) of some type of sporting event. Research a sport that you are interested in and collect the data you will require. The information must be presented in such a way that it will attract the reader's attention and be easy for them to understand.

3.6 DEVELOPMENTS

By the end of this section you should have developed a knowledge and understanding of:

- how to design and make products from various sheet materials based on developments of the following shapes:
  - cubes
  - prisms
  - cylinders
  - pyramids
  - cones.

*A **surface development** (often called a net) is the flat shape that is cut out of a sheet material such as paper, card or thin plastic, and then folded up to make products like packaging, boxes, display stands, cartons and architectural models.*

Methods of producing a development

Cuts, folds and tabs

Most developments have edges that have to be cut or folded, and tabs that have to be glued. Figure 3.82 shows how these different features should be represented on the drawing of a development.

Cube

A **cube** has six square sides (sometimes called surfaces or faces). It is possible to lay out the development of a cube in a number of ways, as shown in Figure 3.83.

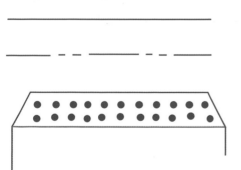

—————————————————   Cut line

— — — — — — — — —   Fold line

Glue tab

Figure 3.82 Cuts, folds and glue tabs

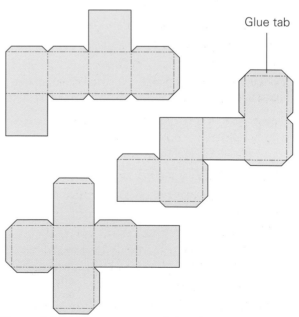

Glue tab

Figure 3.83 Different ways of developing a cube

The three surface developments shown in Fig. 3.83 will all produce the same cube. You would need to choose the one that used the least amount of material to make it, or the one that **tessellated** the best. Which would this be?

You would need seven glue tabs if you wanted to glue all the sides together, but often you would want part of the cube to open, as shown in Figure 3.84.

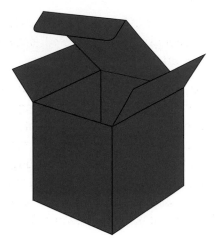

Figure 3.84 Opening box

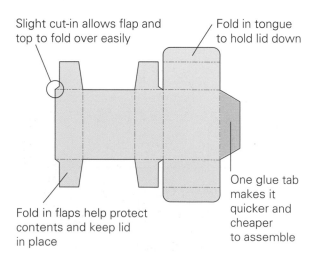

Slight cut-in allows flap and top to fold over easily

Fold in tongue to hold lid down

Fold in flaps help protect contents and keep lid in place

One glue tab makes it quicker and cheaper to assemble

Figure 3.85 What a development looks like

Boxes that open

Figure 3.85 shows the features that need to be included on the development for many types of packaging, such as those shown in Figure 3.86.

Any box that has a square or rectangular bottom can be made from a development that has six sides. Not all these sides would be the same shape or size.

ACTIVITY

Can you work out what the developments required to make the boxes shown in Figure 3.86 would be like? Draw what you think each development would be like, then cut them out and see if you were correct.

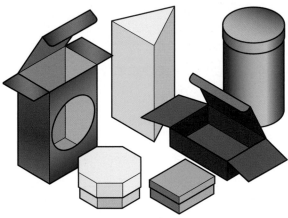

Figure 3.86 Examples of boxes

Prisms

The two ends of a **prism** are the same regular shape. A prism is named after the shape of its end, as shown in Figure 3.87.

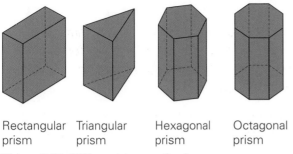

Rectangular prism Triangular prism Hexagonal prism Octagonal prism

Figure 3.87 Different types of prism

The development of any prism can be drawn using the method shown in Figure 3.88.

Stage 1   The plan and front view need to be drawn.

Stage 2   Draw lines across from the front view to give you the height of the prism. Measure the lengths of the sides and draw in the vertical lines. It will help you if you number the corners of the shape in both the plan and the development.

Stage 3   You now need to add the top and bottom (the ends), as well as appropriate glue tabs and fold-in flaps that are required to make the object you require. For example, do you want both the top and bottom to open or just the top? It might even be that you want one of the sides to open and the top and bottom to be glued. There are several variations that you could have with any of the shapes that you will be looking at in this section.

Cylinder

The curved part of a **cylinder** is easily made from a rectangular piece of card, but it can be difficult to attach the circular ends.

The height of the cylinder can be measured and marked on to the card. The length of the development will be the same as the circumference of the cylinder. You can either calculate this or measure it by setting a pair of compasses to the distance across one 30 degree division of the circle and stepping this off 12 times, as shown in Figure 3.89.

If the ends are made from card you need to add a series of very small glue tabs around each of the circles, as shown in Figure 3.90.

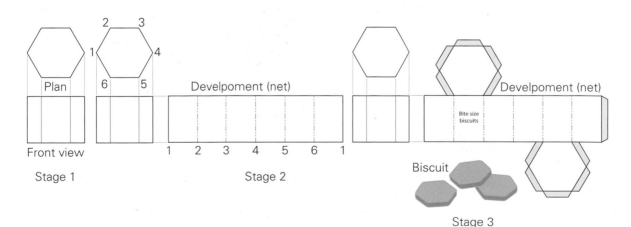

Figure 3.88 Development of a prism

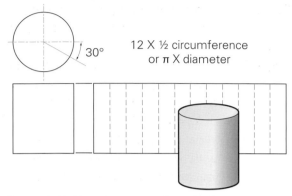

12 X ½ circumference
or π X diameter

30°

Figure 3.89 Development of a cylinder

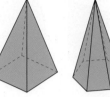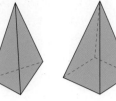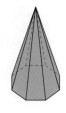

| Triangular pyramid | Rectangular pyramid | Hexagonal pyramid | Octagonal pyramid |

Figure 3.91 Different types of pyramid

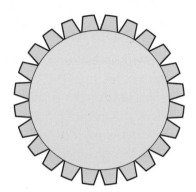

Figure 3.90 Making the end for a cylinder

This can be rather fiddly and you might find it easier to use a thicker material like foam board for the ends. The rectangular strip of card could be glued directly to the edge of the foam board.

Pyramid

A **pyramid** has a regular shape as its base. Sloping edges join the corners of the base to the apex (or top). This is a point directly above the centre of the base. A pyramid is named after the shape of its base, as shown in Figure 3.91.

The development of any type of pyramid can be drawn using the method shown in Figure 3.92.

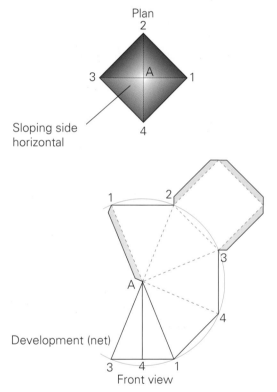

Plan

Sloping side horizontal

Development (net)

Front view

Figure 3.92 Development of a pyramid

Stage 1   The plan and the front view of the pyramid need to be drawn. You must position the plan so that one of the sloping sides is horizontal.

Stage 2   A pair of compasses needs to be set to the length of the sloping side (A-1) on the front view, and an arc drawn with its centre at A. The length of each side needs to be stepped off around the arc. The points can now be joined up.

Stage 3 The base and appropriate glue tabs and fold-in flaps can now be added.

There are other ways of drawing developments for pyramids, as shown in Figure 3.93.

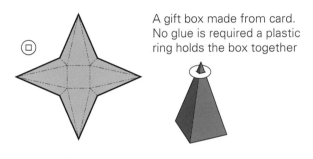

A gift box made from card. No glue is required a plastic ring holds the box together

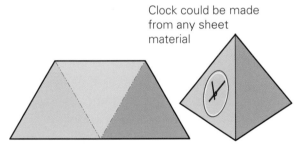

Clock could be made from any sheet material

Figure 3.93 Alternative ways of developing a pyramid

Some of these methods, like the 'star' shape, can result in material being wasted.

Cone

A **cone** has a circular base that slopes up to a single point, the apex.

The development of the sloping surface is easy to draw but, as with the cylinder, it can be difficult to attach the circular base.

Stage 1 Start by drawing the plan and front view of the cone, as shown in Figure 3.94.

Stage 2 Compasses need to be set to the same length as the sloping side in the front view and an arc drawn with its centre at A.

Stage 3 Next the circumference of the base of the cone needs to be measured around this arc. You can do this by setting a pair of compasses to the distance across one 30-degree sector and stepping this off 12 times. A circular base can be added in the same way as for a cylinder.

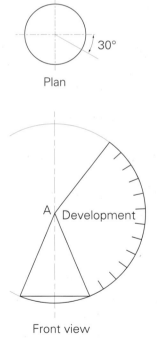

Figure 3.94 Development of a cone

EXAMINER'S TIP

When drawing a development you must always show cut lines, fold lines and, when required, glue tabs and fold-in flaps. Remember, fold-in flaps are wider than glue tabs.

Truncated shapes

The two boxes shown in Figure 3.95 are in the shape of rectangular prisms that have been truncated. This means that part of each shape has been cut off. The top of one box hinges, or 'flips up', while the other lifts off.

The method used to draw the development of a truncated rectangular prism is shown in Figure 3.96.

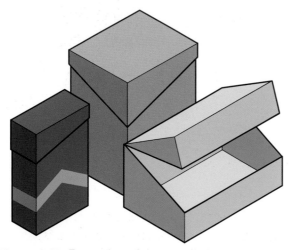

Figure 3.95 Examples of truncated shapes

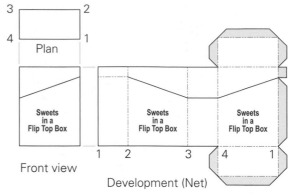

Figure 3.96 Development of a truncated prism

Stage 1	Draw the plan and front view, including the line that shows where the cut has been made.
Stage 2	Lines need to be drawn across from the front view to give the height of the prism, the width of each side of the prism measured 1–2, 2–3, and so on, and the vertical edges drawn.
Stage 3	Lines are drawn across from the front view at the points where the edges are cut. Numbering each corner makes it easier to work out where the cut line goes. For example, you can follow corner 3 on the plan down to the cut on the front view and then across horizontally until it meets edge 3 on the development, as shown in Figure 3.96.
Stage 4	Appropriate glue tabs are added.

This method can be used for any type of truncated prism or cylinder, as shown in Figure 3.97 – you just have more lines to deal with.

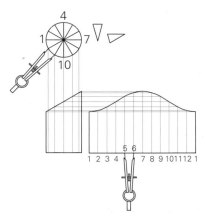

Figure 3.97 Truncated cylinder

 EXAMINER'S TIPS

- Truncated shapes are useful when you want to have an opening lid that is attached to a box.
- Remember to consider how the lid will be secured when closed.

Truncated pyramids, like the container for popcorn shown in Figure 3.98, and truncated cones can be developed by adopting a method very similar to the one used for a complete pyramid or cone.

The method is explained in Figure 3.99. If you number the corners on both the plan and the development you can follow a number from the plan down to the front view and round on to the development until it crosses the line with the same number. This gives you a point on the cut line. Plotting further points and joining them up enables you to complete the cut line.

Figure 3.98 Container for popcorn

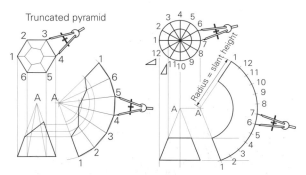

Figure 3.99 Truncated pyramid and cone

Slot and tab fixings

While many surface developments are glued together, there are occasions when a less permanent method of joining is required.

Slot and **tab** fixings allow part or all of a product to be assembled and disassembled without causing damage to the product.

Three of the more common types of slot and tab fixings are shown in Figure 3.100.

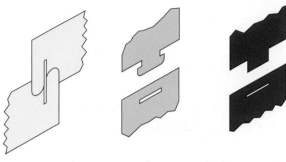

Locking tabs | Locking tab (tongue) pushes through slot and locks into place | Tab (tongue) slides into slot

Figure 3.100 Common slot and tab fixings

This method of joining is commonly used on packaging where you need to be able to open and securely close part of it, as shown in Figure 3.101.

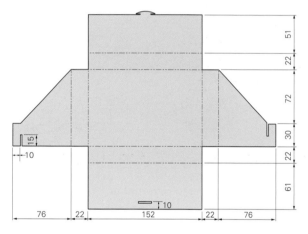

Figure 3.101 Packaging with slot and locking tab

Products such as the leaflet holder shown in Figure 3.102 and point-of-sale display stands are frequently joined together with slot and tab fixings.

This enables them to be sent flat-packed and assembled later, which makes them less costly for the manufacturer to produce as there are no assembly costs. The items are easier and cheaper to transport and store

because they take up less space and are not so likely to be damaged.

ACTIVITY
(a) Draw the net for the packaging shown in Figure 3.101.
(b) Using ICT, design a label to go on the packaging. It does not have to be for a chocolate bar – perhaps you can think of another product that would fit into the packaging.

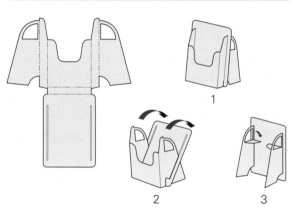

Figure 3.102 Leaflet holder

KEY POINTS

- Adjacent edges on a development must be the same size so that it can be assembled correctly.

- Lettering and other surface detail must be positioned correctly so that it is the right way up when assembled.

- There must be sufficient glue tabs or other methods of fixing to hold the development together when assembled.

EXAMINER'S TIPS

- Some types of slot and tab fixings do not hold the two parts together securely, resulting in them opening or coming apart easily. You need to make sure that the method you use is suitable for a particular situation.
- You could be asked to complete a development that has been started in the question.
- You may be asked to draw the development of an object that you are given information about in the question.
- A question could require you to design a product for a given situation that requires a net to be constructed.
- Features such as fold lines and glue tabs always need to be clearly identified.

KEY TERMS

CONE – object with a circular base tapering to a point
CUBE – a three-dimensional object with six equal square surfaces
CYLINDER – object with straight sides and circular ends
PRISM – three-dimensional object with ends that are the same shape
PYRAMID – object with sloping triangular sides that meet at the top
SLOT – a narrow opening through which something is to be put
SURFACE DEVELOPMENT – The shape of a piece of sheet material from which a three-dimensional object can be formed
TAB – small projecting piece of material
TESSELLATE – in industry, developments are arranged on a sheet with as small a gap as possible between them; this is called a tessellation pattern and avoids waste

ACTIVITY

1. Collect examples of different ways in which boxes open. For example, hinged tops with tuck-in flaps and lift-off lids. Take photographs of what you have collected, stick them on a sheet of A3 paper and add some sketches and notes to explain how each example works. This will make a good reference sheet when you are producing your own designs. You can do a similar activity for features such as joining methods that do not require glue, different types of bases or different ideas for cut-out windows.

2. Make a series of drawings of the outside of your house or part of your school. Work out what developments you would need and make a scale model of your chosen building.

3. Design and make a one-piece development for a leaflet holder that can join together without the use of glue or any other additional materials.

4. Design and make a piece of packaging to hold an MP3 player and its accessories.

5. Take pieces of packaging apart to see how they are made. Record your results using photographs, notes and sketches.

3.7 MODEL MAKING AND PRODUCT MANUFACTURE

LEARNING OUTCOMES

By the end of this section you should have developed a knowledge and understanding of:

- fabrication
- vacuum forming
- line bending
- adhesives.

In addition to developments, you need to know about a range of other processes that can be used to make models and products from graphic materials.

Joining and shaping graphic materials

Fabrication

Fabrication involves joining two or more separate pieces together, as shown in Figure 3.103. You need to know how to fabricate part or all of a product from foam board, corrugated plastic, thick card and thin plastic sheet.

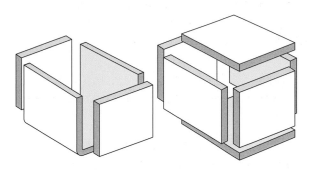

Figure 3.103 Examples of simple fabrication

Foam board

Foam board is one of the best graphic materials from which to fabricate products. It can be joined and shaped in various ways, as shown in Figure 3.104.

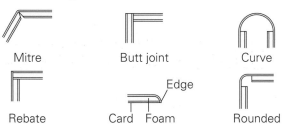

Mitre Butt joint Curve

Rebate Card Foam Edge Rounded

Figure 3.104 Ways of joining and shaping foam board

For some of the techniques shown above you have to be very careful not to cut through the paper layers on the foam board.

PVA glue can be used to join the pieces of foam board together. Masking tape is a good way of holding the pieces in place until the glue dries.

Foam board is particularly useful for making architectural models like the part finished design for a house shown in Figure 3.105.

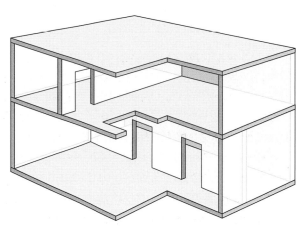

Figure 3.105 Model of a house

Corrugated plastic (sometimes called corriflute or correx)

This is another material that is useful for both model making and the production of various products such as the 'house for sale' sign shown in Figure 3.106, which has been fabricated from two pieces of corrugated plastic.

Figure 3.106 House for sale board

The material is easy to cut and can be folded in the direction of the flutes. Common methods of joining include glue, slots and tabs or 'click' rivets. For example, the rectangular shape on the house for sale board could be attached to the background by click rivets, enabling it to be taken off, turned over to read 'Sold', and re-attached.

Pieces of corrugated plastic can also be joined by lengths of metal or plastic rod, which are pushed into the flutes. Angled corners can be achieved by bending the rod.

Thick card and thin plastic sheet

Both these materials can be fabricated by using butt joints, which are glued together. Plastic sheet is particularly useful when you require a curved surface such as the one shown in Figure 3.103.

All the materials you have looked at in this section can be fabricated using cross-halving joints, as shown in Figure 3.107.

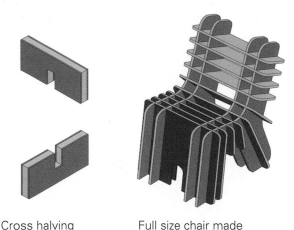

Cross halving

Full size chair made by fabricating pieces of corrugated cardboard using cross halving joints

Figure 3.107 Cross-halving joint

The slot should be the same width as the thickness of the material going into it. The slot is removed from the bottom half of one piece and the top half of the other piece.

Any appropriate combination of materials can be used when fabricating a model or an actual product.

EXAMINER'S TIP

Always make sure that your choice of fabrication method is appropriate to both the material and the situation.

KEY TERM

FABRICATION – making an object from several pieces of material

ACTIVITY

(a) Design a facility where students who cycle to school could keep their bikes. The facility should have a roof but no sides.
(b) Using fabrication techniques, produce a model of your design.

Vacuum forming

Vacuum forming is the process used to form thin plastic sheet into products such as blister packs or the inserts to go inside packaging to hold the contents in place (see Figure 3.108).

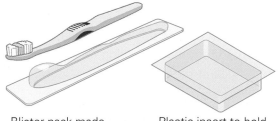

Blister pack made by vacuum forming

Plastic insert to hold a computer game made by vacuum forming

Figure 3.108 Blister pack and plastic insert

Making the mould

You need to make a mould over which the plastic shape will be formed. Usually the mould is made from wood but fine detail can be achieved by cutting out and gluing pieces of card to the top of the finished wooded mould. The sides of the mould must have a slight slope on them and all of the corners need to be rounded as shown in Figure 3.109. This will allow the formed plastic to be removed from the mould easily, and avoid the possibility of sharp corners puncturing the plastic.

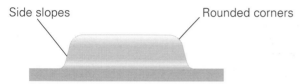

Figure 3.109 Mould for vacuum forming

The process of vacuum forming

A thermoplastic such as high-impact polystyrene (HIPS) is used for vacuum forming. The process is explained in Figure 3.110.

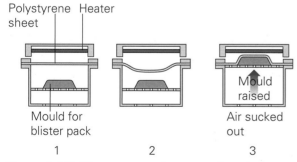

Figure 3.110 The process of vacuum forming

Stage 1   The mould is positioned in the vacuum **former** and the sheet of polystyrene is clamped above it.

Stage 2   The plastic is heated until it becomes soft and flexible. At this

stage it first sags and then goes flat. It is now ready to be vacuum formed.

Stage 3   The mould is raised and the vacuum pump turned on. The air is sucked out and atmospheric pressure forces the plastic sheet down on to the mould. When the plastic has cooled down it can be removed from the mould and cut to the required shape.

Line bending

Polystyrene sheet can be bent to any angle easily using a strip heater (sometimes called a line bender).

A strip heater has an electric heating element mounted under a narrow opening, as shown in Figure 3.111.

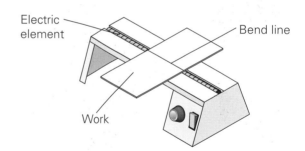

Figure 3.111 Strip heater

Stage 1   Start by marking the position of the bend on to the plastic.

Stage 2   Place the bend line over the heat and wait until the plastic becomes soft. At this stage the plastic needs to be placed in an appropriate former and allowed to cool.

A former for creating a right-angled bend is shown in Figure 3.112.

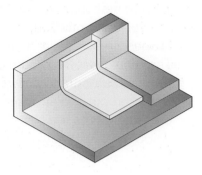

Figure 3.112 Jig for forming plastic

Many shapes, such as the menu holder shown in Figure 3.113, can be made using the **line (strip) bending** process.

Figure 3.113 Menu holder

EXAMINER'S TIP

Practise producing fully labelled diagrams that explain how to vacuum form and line bend thermosetting plastic sheet.

KEY TERMS

FORMER – an object around which materials can be shaped

LINE (STRIP) BENDING – a process where a sheet of thermoplastic can be heated and bent to various angles and curves

VACUUM FORMING – a method of shaping plastic sheet by heating it until it softens. It is then pulled down over a mould by the vacuum created under the mould

ACTIVITY

1. (a) Design and make a blister pack in which a piece of jewellery could be sold.
   (b) Explain, stage by stage, how the blister pack could be made.

2. (a) Design and make a menu holder similar to, but not the same as, the one shown in Figure 3.113.
   (b) Design a former to help you bend the plastic.
   (c) Explain, stage by stage, how the menu holder could be made.

▌ Adhesives

You need to be able to make informed choices about which is the most suitable type of **adhesive** to use when joining materials together.

PVA adhesive

Polyvinyl acetate (PVA) is excellent for gluing card, wood, foam board and rigid-foam

Styrofoam™. You should avoid using it on paper as it tends to make it wrinkle. The glue is white but dries clear in about 2–3 hours. It is safe to use but you should avoid contact with eyes and skin.

Spray adhesive (spray mount)

This adhesive comes in an aerosol can. It will not stain, soak or wrinkle even very thin paper. It is a quick and very effective way of mounting drawings and photographs as it dries very quickly. It can, however, be messy to use and care needs to be taken to cover the area around the item being sprayed. Spray adhesive must be used in a well-ventilated area or in a spray booth with an extractor system, as shown in Figure 3.114.

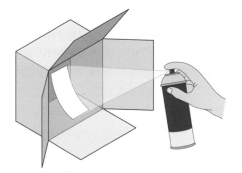

Figure 3.114 Spray booth

Polystyrene cement

This usually comes in a tube and is suitable for joining pieces of polystyrene sheet together. This glue dries very quickly and gives a clear finish. Polystyrene cement must be used in a well-ventilated area.

Solvent (or tensol) cement

Acrylic can be joined to itself using **solvent** cement. This liquid adhesive is applied using either a small brush or an eye-dropper nozzle. The solvent cement welds the two pieces of acrylic together by causing the surface of the acrylic to momentarily liquidise before

hardening again. Solvent cement can be an irritant to both eyes and skin. Goggles and gloves should be worn and the adhesive must only be used in a well-ventilated area or in a spray booth with an extraction system.

Glue gun

You can buy glue guns in either a 'hot melt' or a 'cool melt' version. If touched the hot glue can burn the skin, therefore the 'cold melt' version is safer to use.

Glue sticks are put into the back end of the glue gun, as shown in Figure 3.115. As you pull the trigger the stick goes into the gun, where it is heated electronically and comes out of the nozzle in the form of a thick liquid. The glue cools down and solidifies very quickly.

Figure 3.115 Glue gun

Because the glue sticks are available in different colours they can be used to create various decorative effects as well as to glue surfaces together.

This method of gluing can be used to join various materials but is least successful on those that have smooth, shiny surfaces.

Epoxy resin

This type of glue is often known by its trade name, Araldite®. It comes in two tubes: one contains the glue and the other the hardener.

The two parts are mixed together to form an adhesive that will join most materials together. It is best to use the quick-setting version, which starts to harden in about 5 minutes. It is advisable to wear gloves and goggles and work in a well-ventilated area when using this product.

Glue sticks

Sometimes known by the trade name Pritt Stick®, glue sticks are one of the most readily available forms of adhesive. They are relatively inexpensive, and are easy, clean and safe to use.

However, glue sticks produce a fairly weak bond, which is fine for gluing paper together or gluing paper to card but is less effective when gluing pieces of card together.

You should always try joining two test pieces together to see how well a particular method works before using it on the actual product you are making.

KEY TERMS

ADHESIVE – a substance that sticks things together
SOLVENT – a chemical that will dissolve the surface of a material

ACTIVITY

Devise, carry out and record some simple tests to explore the strength of different adhesives when used on graphic materials. Keep your results as a reference sheet for use when designing and making. It will enable you to make more informed choices about which adhesive would be the most appropriate to use in a given situation.

3.8 MECHANICAL SYSTEMS

LEARNING OUTCOMES

By the end of this section you should have developed a knowledge and understanding of:

- what a mechanism is
- how a mechanism transforms an input motion into a desired output motion and force
- linear, reciprocating, rotary and oscillating motion
- levers and linkages
- V-fold pop-up systems
- multi-layer pop-up systems.

Understanding how mechanical systems work will enable you to produce a range of interactive graphic products such as pop-up cards and books, educational toys and activities, as well as promotional products that include an element of 'surprise'.

▶ Types of motion, movement and pivots

What is a mechanism?

A **mechanism** involves some kind of movement.

Most mechanisms consist of several moving parts (often called a mechanical system). As you move one part of the mechanism (the input motion) it makes another part move in a different way (the output motion).

Look at the page from a child's **interactive** book shown in Figure 3.116.

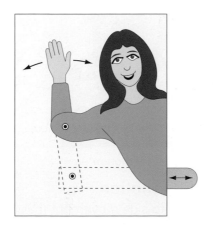

Figure 3.116 Page from a child's interactive book

When the child pushes and pulls the tab that sticks out from the edge of the page, it makes the arm swing from side to side. The mechanism is all the moving parts.

ACTIVITY

(a) Look at existing graphic products that include movement. Take photographs and find out what mechanism(s) have been used to make them work.

(b) Stick the photographs on a sheet of A3 paper, and add notes and sketches to explain how the mechanisms work and what type of motion is created. This will be a good reference sheet when you are designing and making your own mechanisms.

Linear motion

A movement that takes place in a straight line in one direction is called linear motion.

A basic mechanism has been used to make the hot air balloon shown in Figure 3.117 move vertically upwards in a straight line when the tab is pulled. The balloon moves with a linear motion.

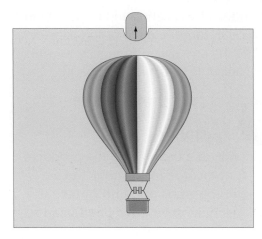

Figure 3.117 Linear motion

EXAMINER'S TIP

You will need to be able to name and describe each type of motion and the movement involved. Your answers will need to be more technical than 'up and down' or 'round and round'.

Reciprocating motion

Reciprocating motion occurs when there is repeated forward and backward movement in a straight line.

For example, the tongue of the clown shown in Figure 3.118 moves in and out of the mouth when the tab is pushed and pulled. The tongue moves with a reciprocating motion.

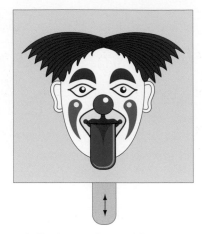

Figure 3.118 Reciprocating motion

Rotary motion

Movement in a circular direction around a central pivot is called rotary motion. The bow tie shown in Figure 3.119 spins round and round as the disc at the edge of the page is rotated. The bow tie moves with a rotary motion.

Figure 3.119 Rotary motion

Oscillating motion

This is a side-to-side movement that follows an arc (part of a circle). The arm of the girl shown in Figure 3.116 swings from side to side. The arm moves with an oscillating motion.

Lever

A **lever** is a length of rigid material, such as card, with a pivot (or fulcrum) somewhere along it. The lever rotates about the pivot point, as shown in Figure 3.120.

By putting the pivot in different positions you can increase or decrease the amount of movement that takes place at each end of the lever.

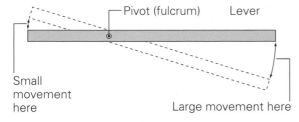

Figure 3.120 Simple lever and pivot

By arranging the input, output and pivot in different ways you can create the three kinds (or classes) of lever shown in Figure 3.121.

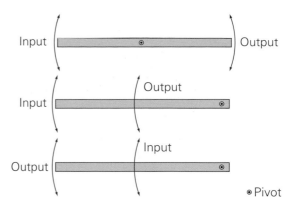

Figure 3.121 Different types of lever

Linkages

Linkages like the one shown in Figure 3.122 are made by joining two or more levers together with pivots. There are two types of pivot that are used. A fixed pivot attaches the linkage to the background, while a movable pivot joins two parts of the linkage together.

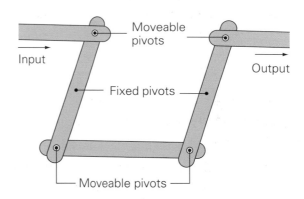

Figure 3.122 Linkage with fixed and movable pivots

Linkages like the ones shown in Figure 3.123 can be used to change the direction of a movement or to change one type of motion into another.

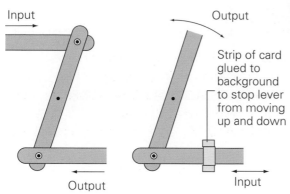

Figure 3.123 Linkages that bring about changes in direction and movement

It is possible to have more than one part of a linkage moving at the same time, as shown in Figure 3.124.

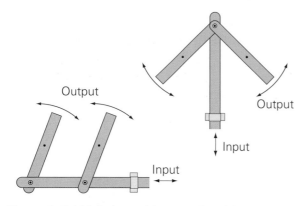

Figure 3.124 Linkages with several moving parts

ACTIVITY

One of these linkages could be used to make the wings of a bird go up and down. The other could be used for a football supporter with their arms above their head waving a scarf from side to side.

(a) Which linkage could be used for which situation?
(b) Try making each of these mechanisms.

EXAMINER'S TIP

- Use notes to explain your ideas.
- Always label pivot points and use arrows to show how the mechanism moves.

Pivots

When making mechanisms from card or thin plastic sheet you can use paper fasteners, eyelets, and click or ratchet rivets as **pivots** (see Figure 3.125).

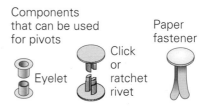

Figure 3.125 Components that can be used for pivots

The position of the pivot is very important in all linkage mechanisms. It can affect how much the mechanism moves and which direction it moves in.

By making slots in appropriate positions it is often possible to hide most of the mechanism behind the background, as shown in Figure 3.126.

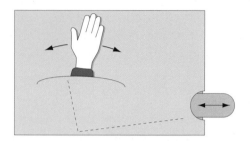

Figure 3.126 Slots to hide the mechanism

By joining levers to other shapes, such as the circular disc shown in Figure 3.127, it is possible to increase the range of movements you can create. In this example it depends how far the lever is pushed and pulled. The disc will either oscillate or rotate.

Creating other types of movement

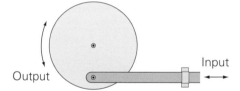

Figure 3.127 Creating other types of movement

 EXAMINER'S TIPS

- Do not always try to invent totally new mechanisms. Generally you can base your answers on mechanisms that you have made or seen.
- You should not make your designs too complicated.
- Try to use graphic materials such as foam board and card rather than inappropriate ones such as string and large amounts of wood and plastic.

 KEY TERMS

LEVER – a simple rigid 'bar' that rotates about a fixed point (a pivot)
LINKAGE – a mechanism involving two or more levers joined together
MECHANISM – creates movement within a product
PIVOT – a point of rotation

Pop-up systems

Pop-ups can create impact and surprise, as well as making products like greeting cards and books more interactive, appealing and interesting to the user.

V-fold pop-up systems

The mechanism gets its name from the V shape that it forms, as shown in Figure 3.128. It is one of the easiest ways of creating a pop-up movement.

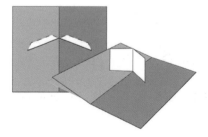

Figure 3.128 V-fold mechanism

To make the mechanism pop up when the book or card is opened it must be arranged symmetrically along the fold line as shown in Figure 3.129.

Figure 3.129 Positioning the V-fold mechanism

You can use several V-folds in order to give your design a more three-dimensional appearance, as shown in Figure 3.130.

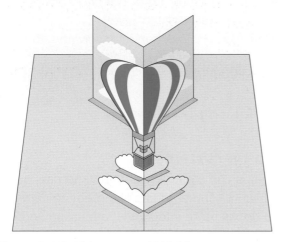

Figure 3.130 Using several V-folds

You must always make sure that all of the design will fit inside the book or card when it is closed.

Multiple-layer pop-up systems

The **multiple**-layer pop-up method is based on parallelograms. Each parallelogram is connected to the page by glue tabs that keep it parallel to the surfaces of the book or card when it is opened at 90 degrees, as shown in Figure 3.131.

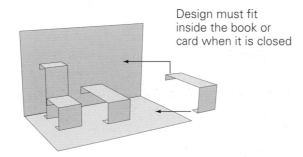

Design must fit inside the book or card when it is closed

Figure 3.131 Multiple layers

A number of parallelograms of different sizes can give the appearance of depth and

distance. Images can either be drawn or stuck on to the vertical surfaces, as shown in Figure 3.132.

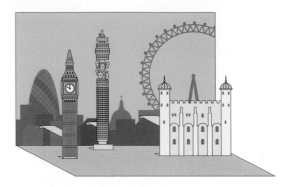

Figure 3.132 Finished multiple-layer pop-up design

You do not necessarily have to make this type of pop-up from separate pieces.

Figure 3.133 shows how it is possible to cut out the shapes from the background.

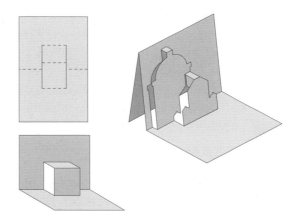

Figure 3.133 One-piece design

You must always make sure that all of the design will fit inside the book or card when it is closed.

EXAMINER'S TIP

All measurements and the 90-degree angles on parallelogram pop-ups must be accurate or the card/page will not close correctly.

ACTIVITY

1. Design and make a pop-up guide to a local museum.

2. Design and make a pop-up menu for children's meals at a local restaurant.

KEY TERMS

INTERACTIVE – two things (in this case the reader and the book) reacting with one another; for example, the person opens the book, the book pops up
MULTIPLE – several

3.9 COMMERCIAL PRINTING PROCESSES

LEARNING OUTCOMES

By the end of this section you should have developed a knowledge and understanding of:

• offset lithography, to include colour separation, process colours CMYK, the order of applying the colours, registration marks, colour bars and crop marks

• digital printing

• flexography.

In school you will have access to low-volume printing methods such as a computer printer and a photocopier. You also need to know how graphic products are printed using industrial processes.

Figure 3.134 Printing a test page

Registration marks

Registration marks are cross-haired lines, as shown in Figure 3.134, that help to ensure that a set of printing plates is lining up accurately (or in register) on the printing press and producing a clearly defined colour image. Registration marks appear in exactly the same place on each printing plate. If a job is 'out of register', there will be a blurring of the edges of the images, as shown in Figure 3.135. Many modern printing presses have sensors that can automatically detect registration marks and ensure registration.

Figure 3.135 Blurred image

Colour bars

The colour bar is a band of CMYK squares running along one end of the printed sheet, as shown in Figure 3.134. This bar is used to ensure that each colour is the correct density.

Crop marks

Crop marks are lines on a printed artwork or a completed print job to indicate where the work should be trimmed (see Figure 3.134).

Offset lithography

Offset lithography is one of the most common forms of commercial printing. It uses the principle that oil and water do not mix.

Graphic design software is used to produce the artwork. An imagesetter is then used to produce films from which the printing plates are made using a photochemical process. A separate plate is produced for each of the process colours.

Cyan is usually printed first, then magenta, followed by yellow and then black.

The image on the plate is designed to attract the ink and will repel water, while the non-image areas are designed to absorb moisture and repel ink.

The flexible plates, which can be made from a variety of materials including aluminium, are attached to the printing press. During printing the plate is kept wet so that ink sticks only to the image areas.

The inked image is first transferred from the plate to a rubber-surfaced blanket roller and from there on to the paper, as shown in Figure 3.136. This indirect method of printing is the 'offset' from which the process gets its name. The rubber roller is flexible enough to both protect the surface of the printing plate and be able to mould to the surface of textured paper.

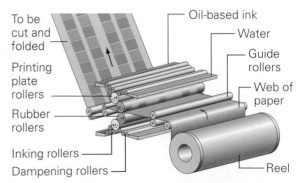

Figure 3.136 The process of offset lithographic printing

EXAMINER'S TIP

Practise producing fully labelled diagrams that explain how commercial printing processes work.

Almost any image can be printed on to paper and card using offset lithography. While it is possible to print on to plastic and metal it is a more difficult process.

It is important that quality control is always monitored by checking registration marks and **colour bars**.

The paper can either be fed to the printing press one set at a time (sheet fed) or from a large roll of paper (**web fed**).

Sheet fed

Pre-cut paper – usually between A4 and A0 in size – is fed as individual sheets in to the printing press. Print runs of about 5000 copies are generally considered viable. However, using a small machine and disposable plates to print single-colour products such as letterheads and business cards, a number as low as 100 might be economical.

Web fed

Material costs can be lower because a continuous roll of paper is cheaper than pre-cut sheets. It does, however, take a long time to set these machines up. To be economical they need to be used for the full-colour printing of products such as magazines and packaging. Print runs of tens of thousands are required.

Process colours

With offset lithography, a full-colour image is produced using four printing plates each applying a different colour. These are called the 'process colours' or CMYK. The **process colours** are cyan (C), magenta (M), yellow (Y) and black (K, Key).

Because the inks are translucent they can be overprinted in a variety of different proportions to produce a wide range of colours, as shown in Figure 3.137.

It is possible to produce an adequate range of colours using cyan, magenta and yellow, but the black strengthens the shadow areas and reduces the amount of the other coloured inks required.

Figure 3.137 Printing a full-colour image

ACTIVITY

Figure 3.138 shows a test that you can do with three pieces of coloured acetate. The test will show you how the process of using the three primary colours of blue (cyan), red (magenta) and yellow to produce a range of other colours, works.

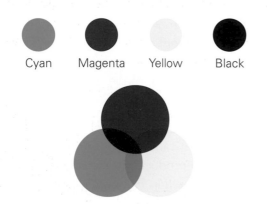

Cyan   Magenta   Yellow   Black

Figure 3.138 Testing how the process works

EXAMINER'S TIP

Make sure you know at least some of the technical terms used in commercial printing processes and the correct names of the colours involved.

Digital printing

This type of printing eliminates the need for making printing plates as a computer is linked directly to the printing machine, as shown in Figure 3.139.

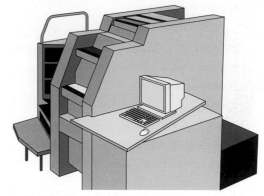

Figure 3.139 Digital printing

This makes it an excellent method for rapid prototyping and also means it is cost-effective for small **print runs**. Up to 250 copies per minute can be produced using **digital printing**. The system comes with a range of features such as image clean-up, enlargement and reduction, photo screening, masking, cropping, and rotating and moving images and text.

It is possible to make every image printed on to paper different as opposed to having to make hundreds or thousands of identical images from one set of printing plates.

Digital printing produces less waste in terms of the chemicals used and the time required to set up the equipment and check such things as colour registration.

The ink used does not soak into the product being printed but forms a thin layer on the surface. This could be considered to make the product easier to recycle.

Digital printing is ideal for personalised printing such as the child's book shown in Figure 3.140, which has been customised with a specific child's name. The name can easily be changed and another copy of the book printed.

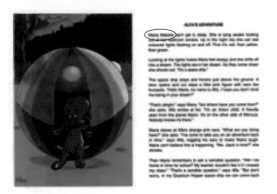

Figure 3.140 Book personalised with child's name

Flexography

Flexography is used with products such as corrugated containers, folding cartons, paper sacks, plastic carrier bags, milk and juice cartons, sweet wrappers and labels (see Figure 3.141).

Figure 3.141 Products printed using flexography

In fact, during the last two decades flexography has become the most dominant form of printing used for packaging. This is largely due to lower quality expectations on the part of customers and the significantly lower cost of production in comparison to other forms of printing. Another influencing factor has been the advances made in flexographic printing. Both the material used for the printing plates and the method of production, either by chemical etching or by laser engraving, have got better.

A flexible plate, which has the images to be printed raised from its surface, is produced and attached to the plate cylinder. The material to be printed is fed in to the printing press on a roll as shown in Figure 3.142. Ink is transferred from the fountain roller to the anilox roller, which has a dimpled surface that transfers the ink to the plate and finally on to the material to be printed with the help of the impression cylinder.

As with offset lithography, each stage of the process prints a single colour. The various tones and shading are achieved by overlaying the four colours of ink.

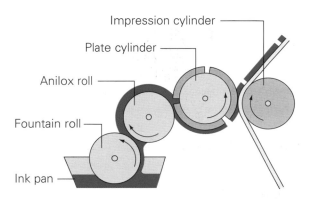

Figure 3.142 The process of flexographic printing

Flexography has an advantage over offset lithography in that it can use a wider range of inks, water based rather than oil based, and is good for printing on a variety of different materials. The inks used have a low viscosity, meaning faster drying and therefore quicker production, resulting in lower costs.

EXAMINER'S TIP

Volume of production, quality and cost are the main factors to consider when choosing a printing method.

KEY TERMS

COLOUR BARS – bars of colour around a printed image to check the density of the colours being printed

CROP MARKS – marks incorporated in a printed sheet to indicate where the paper is to be trimmed or cut to size

DIGITAL PRINTING – a system where the printing press is directly linked to a computer, so there is no need to produce printing plate; designs can easily be customised and changed

FLEXOGRAPHY – used to print cartons, packaging and point-of-sale materials; used for long print runs at low costs

OFFSET LITHOGRAPHY – image is not printed direct from a plate but 'offset' first on to a rubber-covered cylinder (the blanket), which performs the printing operation; the system is based on the principle of water and oil not mixing; generally used for long print runs

PRINT RUN – the number of copies to be printed at one time

PROCESS COLOURS – cyan (a shade of blue), magenta (a shade of red), yellow and black, which are combined in four-colour printing processes to produce a full-colour image

REGISTRATION MARKS – crossed lines printed around the edge of a design that need to line up when each colour is applied, in order to create a clear image

WEB FED – printing on to a continuous roll of paper rather than single sheets

ACTIVITY

1. (a) Collect a range of different printed materials. Produce a sample sheet that identifies the product, the material and the method of printing used for each.
   (b) Comment on the quality of printing and any faults that you can find.
   (c) Compare the examples of printing that you have collected with examples that you have produced using school-based facilities such as photocopying and a computer printer.

2. Using the internet to help you, produce a short resource booklet that provides information about the commercial printing methods you need to be familiar with.

3.10 LABELLING

By the end of this section you should have developed a knowledge and understanding of:

- a range of symbols and pictograms associated with recycling and environmental issues.

*Manufacturers are committed to promoting **recycling** and the use of recycled materials. The examples shown are some of the symbols and pictograms that appear on products and packaging to advise consumers about recycling issues and to promote environmental claims.*

The Recycle Mark

The Recycle Mark, shown in Figure 3.143, is a call for action, encouraging people to recycle wherever possible.

Figure 3.143 The Recycle Mark

The new packaging symbols

These incorporate the Recycle Mark in their design and are starting to appear on packaging from some of the major brands. They help to identify how the different parts of the packaging can be recycled.

On the example shown in Figure 3.144, 'Widely Recycled' means at least 65% of people have access to recycling facilities for this material.

'Check Locally' means 15%–65% of people have access to recycling facilities for this material.

'Not Recycled' means that fewer than 15% of people have access to recycling facilities for this material.

HEADER

| CARD | FOIL | PLASTIC |
| widely recycled | check local recycling | not currently recycled |

Figure 3.144 The new packaging symbols

The green dot

This symbol, shown in Figure 3.145, is used on packaging in many European countries and indicates that the manufacturer has contributed towards the cost of recycling the packaging.

Figure 3.145 The green dot

The mobius loop

This is the international recycling symbol. It is made up of three chasing arrows, as shown in Figure 3.146, and indicates that a product can be recycled.

Figure 3.146 The mobius loop

The mobius loop with a percentage

This symbol, shown in Figure 3.147, is found on cardboard. The 'x' in the centre of the loop shows what percentage of the material is recycled.

Figure 3.147 Mobius loop with a percentage

Paper

To be given the National Association of Paper Merchants' mark, shown in Figure 3.148, paper or board must be made from a minimum of 75% genuine waste paper and/or board fibre. The percentage in the centre denotes the proportion of recycled material in the product.

Figure 3.148 National Association of Paper Merchants' mark

SPI symbols

These symbols, shown in Figure 3.149, are used on plastics that can be recycled after use if suitable collection facilities exist. The specific type of plastic is identified by the numbers 1–7. For example, plastic milk bottles have the symbol with the number 2 inside. They are made from HDPE: high-density polyethylene.

Figure 3.149 SPI symbols

Glass

The pictogram shown in Figure 3.150 means 'Please put this in a bottle bank'. It is to remind people to recycle glass bottles and jars either in a bottle bank or using kerbside collection.

Figure 3.150 'Please put this in a bottle bank'

Aluminium

The symbol shown in Figure 3.151 indicates that the packaging is made from aluminium, which can be recycled using either a can bank or kerbside collection.

Figure 3.151 Recyclable aluminium

Steel

Recyclable steel is indicated using the pictogram shown in Figure 3.152. It can be recycled either using a can bank or kerbside collection.

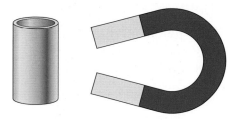

Figure 3.152 Recyclable steel

Compostable plastic packaging

This symbol, shown in Figure 3.153, is used on plastic packaging that is biodegradable. This type of packaging has recently been introduced for products such as organic fruit and vegetables.

Figure 3.153 Compostable plastic

Tidyman

The Tidyman or 'Do not litter' symbol, shown in Figure 3.154, encourages people to dispose of unwanted packaging carefully and thoughtfully. This does not directly relate to recycling but is a reminder to be a good citizen by disposing of your rubbish in the most appropriate way.

KEEP BRITAIN TIDY

Figure 3.154 Tidyman symbol

Eco-labelling

This is a voluntary system, which is used to identify and label products that have minimal environmental impact.

The design shown in Figure 3.155 is the symbol of the European eco-labelling scheme. The scheme enables manufacturers, retailers and service providers to receive recognition for good practice, and helps consumers to make more informed choices.

Figure 3.156 Carbon footprint

Figure 3.155 European eco-label

EXAMINER'S TIP

Green design and eco-design are common themes for test questions.

Carbon footprint

A **carbon** footprint label of the type shown in Figure 3.156 indicates the amount of CO_2 and other greenhouse gases emitted as part of a product's manufacture, distribution, use and disposal – otherwise known as its carbon footprint.

Those companies that label their products and services are committed to reducing their carbon from the figure shown within two years. As more companies take part in carbon reduction labelling, consumers will be able to make more informed choices.

KEY POINT

Recycling helps to conserve the Earth's natural and finite resources by reducing energy use and pollution.

KEY TERMS

CARBON – a chemical element that exists in all living matter
CONVENTION – standard, internationally accepted method of representing something
RECYCLING – reusing waste or unwanted materials

ACTIVITY

(a) Collect various pieces of packaging and cut off the various symbols and pictograms linked with recycling and the environment.

(b) Stick them on a sheet of A3 paper and see how many you can name and write a brief explanation of. This will make a good revision sheet.

CHAPTER 4

COMPUTER APPLICATIONS

4.1 THE USE OF CAD PACKAGES IN SCHOOL

LEARNING OUTCOME

By the end of this section you should have developed a knowledge and understanding of:

- how computer-aided design (CAD) can be used to support design development.

To successfully complete Units A531 and A533 you will need to demonstrate the use of CAD. CAD should be used to support design development and to present final working drawings.

▶ Computer-aided design (CAD)

Computer-aided design (**CAD**) is the use of computer technology to aid in the design, and especially the drafting (technical drawing and engineering drawing), of a part or product. It is a way of turning hand-drawn sketches of initial ideas into neat, scale drawings that show the exact dimensions and proportions of how a product will look. CAD enables designers to lay out and develop work on-screen. The work can be printed and saved for future editing, saving time on drawing.

Drafting can be done in two dimensions (**2D**) and three dimensions (**3D**). 2D drawing is traditionally used to create 'working drawings' similar to those that can be created on a drawing board. Working drawings show views of an object from three different sides. 3D CAD allows you to create an image of a 'whole product' on the screen and view it from all angles by rotating it in three dimensions.

There are many different CAD software packages available, which all work in basically the same way. The CAD software packages commonly used in schools range from 2D vector-based drafting systems such as Techsoft 2D design to more complex and sophisticated 3D solid and surface modelling software such as AutoCAD and ProDesktop.

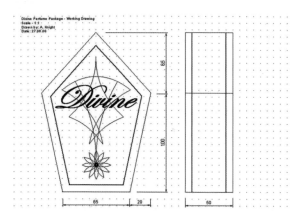

Figure 4.1 Simple 2D drawing

The simple orthographic drawing shown in Figure 4.1 was produced on a 2D vector-based package. It shows the front and side views of a proposed perfume package. This would be used in the later stages of the design process to transfer a final design proposal into a 'working drawing'. The information in the drawing gives enough detail to see the real proportions of the final product. Someone with reasonable manufacturing skills would be able to make the package using the information given.

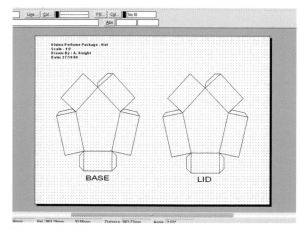

Figure 4.2 2D net

The drawing in Figure 4.2 shows a 2D net of the proposed perfume package produced

using the same program. Using a CAD package to produce the net enables the designer to print it on to paper or card, cut it out and assemble it as either a scale model or a full-size prototype.

A computer-aided manufacturing (CAM) machine, such as a vinyl or laser cutter, could be used to score the fold lines and cut out the net automatically.

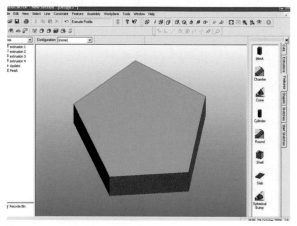

Figure 4.3 3D drawing

The drawing in Figure 4.3 has been produced using a 3D surface modelling program. It shows the same perfume package, but it is represented as a 3D view that can be rotated and viewed from any angle.

Unlike the 2D 'working drawing', this 3D representation does not show dimensions and could not be used to actually produce the item. It does, however, show a more realistic representation of what the final item will actually look like.

Different CAD packages may vary in their methods of producing drawings but they will all have the same basic toolbar and commands. On most packages it is relatively easy to learn the main commands and functions to produce simple drawings and designs. Many have inbuilt tutorials that teach the basics in simple steps, and there are many specialist textbooks available on individual CAD packages. Your teacher should be able to teach you all you will need to know to produce some 2D and 3D drawings of your own designs.

You should use whichever CAD package you have available to you to develop your initial designs, demonstrate your ability to present work using a range of graphical techniques, and clearly communicate details of your chosen design and prototype.

EXAMINER'S TIP

Use CAD to develop your ideas, demonstrate creativity and communicate important details.

KEY TERMS

2D – drawing in two dimensions
3D – drawing in three dimensions
CAD – computer-aided design

KEY POINT

- CAD should be used to develop and refine your designs, *not* to create initial designs.

4.2 ON-SCREEN MODELLING AND ON-SCREEN MANIPULATION

LEARNING OUTCOMES

By the end of this section you should have developed a knowledge and understanding of:

- how graphic image manipulation software can be used to support design development
- computer applications that can be used to manipulate images and model solutions on-screen.

Graphic modelling should be used to support design development throughout the Graphics course. You will need to demonstrate the use of graphic modelling techniques in the controlled assessment units, A531 and A533.

▶ Graphic modelling and on-screen manipulation

This involves editing (altering, modifying and changing) existing graphic images such as photographs, logos and pictures, and creating new images by combining them with items such as other existing images, text and shapes.

Many specialist graphic image manipulation packages (**GIMPs**) are available, which have a wide range of functions and can produce extremely high-quality images. These are specialist packages, which are used by professional designers and can be extremely expensive as well as difficult and time consuming to learn.

However, there are many common software programs freely available in schools that will allow you to perform a number of the more basic editing functions to manipulate images on-screen – such as rotating, cropping, resizing and recolouring.

Regardless of the software package, they are all likely to have similar functions and commands.

Rotating images

You may already have an image stored on your computer. Open a graphics package and insert the image on to the page. On the example shown in the pictures on this page the photo is the wrong way round and needs to be **rotated** anticlockwise through 90 degrees.

Figure 4.4 Select the image by clicking on it

Figure 4.5 Select the rotate command from the relevant menu or icon

Figure 4.6 Rotate the image so it is the correct way up

Cropping images

The image is now the correct way up but has too much background. To correct this, the image needs to be **cropped** to remove the unwanted parts. This is done using the crop command.

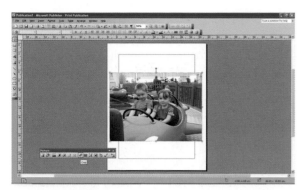

Figure 4.7 Select image; select the crop command from the relevant menu or icon

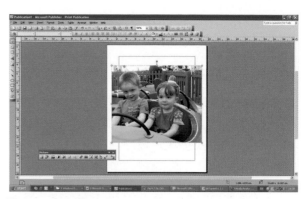

Figure 4.10 Drag to stretch the image to the correct size

By clicking and dragging one of the edge tabs instead of the corners you can stretch the image in one direction only and disproportion it.

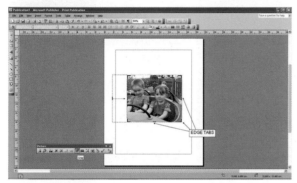

Figure 4.8 Click on the edge tabs; drag to crop the unwanted parts from the image

Stretching and shrinking images

The image has now been cropped, but it is too small and needs to be **resized** in order to make it bigger.

Figure 4.11

Figure 4.9 Select the image by clicking on it, then click on one of the four corner tabs

Figure 4.12

Colour, contrast and brightness

As well as moving, rotating, cropping and stretching an object, you can lighten, darken or totally **recolour** an image.

As well as lightening and darkening you can change or modify the colour of your image by re-colouring or re-formatting it, using preset colours.

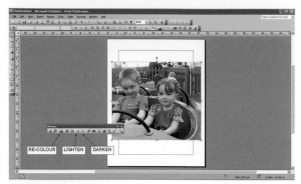

Figure 4.13 Select the image, then select the lighten, darken or recolour command from the relevant menu or icon

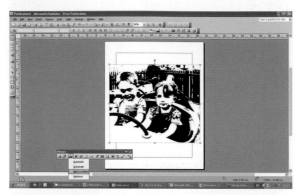

Figure 4.16 Black and white

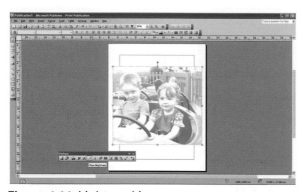

Figure 4.14 Lightened image

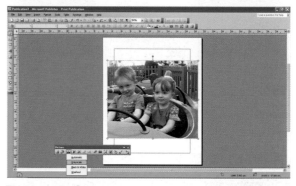

Figure 4.17 Greyscale

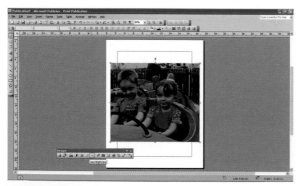

Figure 4.15 Darkened image

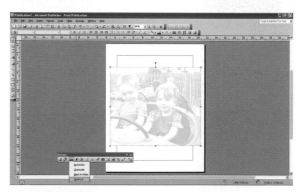

Figure 4.18 Washout/watermark

By using the 'format' and 'recolour picture' commands you can make the image any colour you choose.

Figure 4.19 Select the image, then the 'format picture' and 'recolour picture' commands; then choose a colour

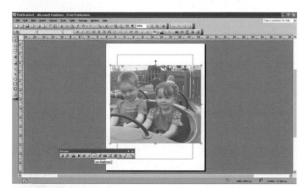

Figure 4.20 Recoloured blue

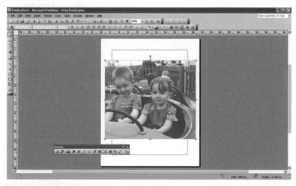

Figure 4.21 Recoloured red

KEY POINT

- GIMPs should be used to develop and refine your designs, *not* to create initial designs.

EXAMINER'S TIP

Use GIMPs to develop your ideas, demonstrate creativity and communicate important details.

KEY TERMS

CROP – remove unwanted parts of an image
GIMP – graphic image manipulation package
RECOLOUR – alter or completely change an image's colour
RESIZE – stretch or shrink an image
ROTATE – turn around

4.3 TEXT, DATABASE AND GRAPHICS SOFTWARE

LEARNING OUTCOME

By the end of this section you should have developed a knowledge and understanding of:

- the uses of text, database and graphics software.

Computer software is a collection of computer programs, procedures and documentation that perform tasks on a computer system. Different types of software have to perform different functions and display information in different ways. You will need to apply and demonstrate knowledge of text, database and graphics software throughout the Graphics course, and particularly in the controlled assessment units, A531 and A533.

Applications software

This type of software program performs productive tasks for the computer user. Examples of this type of software include graphics software, word processing, spreadsheets and databases.

Applications software is often purchased separately from computer hardware, but sometimes applications are bought with the computer. Lots of applications put together as a package are sometimes referred to as an **application suite**. Microsoft Office, which puts together a word processor, a spreadsheet and several other applications, is an example of this.

Applications are almost always separate programs from the computer's operating system. They are often designed and manufactured for use with a specific platform or operating system – for instance, 'Microsoft Office for Windows XP': Microsoft Office is the 'application' but it is designed specifically for Windows XP (Windows XP is the platform, or operating system).

Text software

Text software is the most common of all application software. Text software refers to programs specifically designed to process text, called 'word processors'.

A word processor is a computer application used for the writing, producing, editing, formatting and printing of any sort of text. Modern word processors include functions such as grammar and spellchecking programs, and a wide range of formatting options. Microsoft Word is the most widely used computer word-processing system and the one you are most likely to have in school.

Database software

Database software stores and organises a set of specific data.

A computer database is a structured collection of records or data that is stored in a computer system. This software is known as a 'database management system' (**DBMS**).

Databases can carry out complex searches for different information and provide answers in a fraction of the time it would take to do it manually.

Example

A school database could search for all boys in Year 9 who travel to school by bus. This is a complex search (three searches together):

1. Boys
2. Year 9
3. Travel by bus.

The resulting list of names could then be sorted alphabetically by forename or surname. A variety of different sorting methods (e.g. alphabetically, numerically) is available within database software.

Search results can be printed out in list form or put into pre-formed documents.

Example

The results from the above search could be mail-merged with a letter home so that the names and addresses of all the boys' parents are put on to the letters and printed out automatically.

Spreadsheet software

Spreadsheet programs are also a kind of database management system.

A spreadsheet is a computer application that simulates a paper worksheet. It is in the form of a grid consisting of rows and columns. Each square of the grid is called a cell, into which you can input alphanumeric text or numeric values.

A spreadsheet can also contain formulas. The formulas in each cell can be calculated from the contents of any other cell (or combination of cells) on the same or different spreadsheets.

When one of these cells is changed, the calculations change accordingly.

Spreadsheets are often used for financial information because of their ability to recalculate the entire sheet automatically after a change is made to a single cell.

Graphics software

Graphics software is application software used for graphic design, multimedia development, specialised image development, general image editing, or simply to access graphic files.

Most graphic software includes common functions, creation tools, editing tools, filters and automated rendering modes, but there are many different types of graphic software designed and used for specific applications.

Graphic design software

This is often referred to as desktop publishing software. It is used in graphic design for general image editing and page layouts.

Multimedia development software

Multimedia development applications are graphic software packages with audio, motion and interactivity, such as software for creating and editing electronic presentations (slide presentations), computer simulations and games.

Image development software

Images can be created from scratch with most art software. Specialised software applications are used for more accurate visual effects. These visual effects include those listed below.

- Vector editors: ideal for the solid, crisp lines seen in line art and poster-type effects.
- Digital painting: used for digital painting (representing real brush and canvas textures or handicraft textures such as mosaic or stained glass (e.g. Photo-Paint, Corel Painter).
- Photo editing: designed for rendering with digital painting effects and hand-rendering styles that don't appear computer generated (e.g. Photoshop).
- Photorealistic effects: creating the illusion of a photographed image using 3D modelling and ray tracing features to make images appear photographed.

KEY POINT

- Text, graphics and database software can be used to perform a wide variety of different tasks and functions.

EXAMINER'S TIP

Try to use appropriate text, graphics or database software in your coursework folder whenever appropriate.

KEY TERMS

APPLICATIONS SOFTWARE – programs designed for specific tasks
APPLICATIONS SUITE – a collection of programs (e.g. Microsoft Office)
DBMS – database management system

4.4 STORING AND SHARING DATA

LEARNING OUTCOME

By the end of this section you should have developed a knowledge and understanding of:

- the different methods of storing and sharing data.

Throughout the Graphics course you will need to develop and demonstrate the ability to store and share electronic data appropriately.

Data storage

This involves the recording and storing of information (data). Storage devices may hold information, process information, or both.

Electronic data storage is storage that requires electrical power to store and retrieve the data.

A device that only holds information is called a recording medium (e.g. CD-ROMs, floppy disks, memory sticks, memory cards).

Figure 4.24 A memory stick

Figure 4.22 A CD-ROM

A device that processes information may access either a **removable recording device** or a **permanent component** to store and retrieve information.

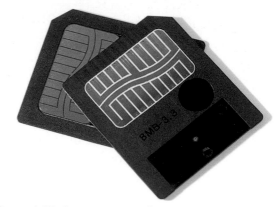

Figure 4.25 A memory card

Figure 4.23 A floppy disk

KEY TERMS

PERMANENT COMPONENT – a computer hard drive
REMOVABLE RECORDING DEVICE – a CD-Rom or floppy disk

Electromagnetic data can be stored in either analogue or digital form on a variety of media. This type of information is called electronically encoded data.

The advantages of storing data electronically are:

- it is easier to search, update and revise

- it is more cost-effective than alternative methods
- it takes up much less physical space (than paper)
- it is easy to replace (rewrite) data.

Figure 4.26 Analogue data: person searching for a file

Storing data on paper takes up lots of room, is time consuming and more difficult to use than **electronic data storage** methods – the amount of data kept on a CD-ROM would fill a number of filing cabinets.

The disadvantages of storing data electronically are:

- electronic storage media are less durable than other, paper-based methods.

This one disadvantage can be overcome by copying (backing up) electronic data, which is very easy to do.

▶ Data sharing

Using computers, data can be shared in a variety of ways. Computer applications have revolutionised the way we can share and transfer data.

Computers can share information on a small, local scale (with a few chosen people), or on a worldwide scale, depending on how many people you want to share your information with.

If you wanted to describe something that had happened to you or something you had done, you could share it in the following ways:

- email the story to a group of friends
- post the information on a website where it could be viewed by anyone on the internet.

Organisations frequently have information they wish to share with all or some of their employees but not with the outside world. This can be done using a local area network (**LAN**), which works in the same way as the internet but shares information only with other computers on the network. By using a LAN, information can be shared in the following ways.

- You can email some or all of the people on the LAN.
- You can post information on the LAN, where it can be viewed by anyone on the LAN.

Many schools have a LAN that links all the computers in the school together and allows communication between all of them, but not the outside world.

Often there are pieces of information on a LAN that only designated people need to have access to (e.g. financial data or databases containing individual employees' personal information). By making certain files or areas on a LAN available only to designated users this data can be restricted to prevent unauthorised access.

Figure 4.27 Image of a LAN

▶ The Data Protection Act

The Data Protection Act (DPA) is a UK Act of Parliament that was introduced in 1998 to protect individuals from having confidential and personal information shared between organisations without their permission.

The Data Protection Act creates rights for those who have their data stored, and responsibilities for those who store or collect personal data.

The person who has their data processed has the right to:

- view the data an organisation holds on them
- request that incorrect information be corrected
- require that data is not used in a way that causes damage or distress
- require that their data is not used for direct marketing.

EXAMINER'S TIP

Use appropriate methods to save and back up your work.

KEY TERMS

ELECTRONIC DATA STORAGE – storing files of any kind using a computer
LAN – local area network

▶ 4.5 APPLICATIONS OF CAD/CAM

LEARNING OUTCOMES

By the end of this section you should have developed a knowledge and understanding of:

- how you can use CAD/CAM to enhance your design and making work.

*As mentioned above, computer-aided design (CAD) is the use of computers in the design, and especially the drafting (technical drawing and engineering drawing), of a part or product. Computer-aided manufacturing (**CAM**) is the use of computer-controlled machine tools to manufacture products drawn using CAD programs.*

▶ Computer-aided manufacturing (CAM)

In simple terms, CAM creates real-life versions of components designed using CAD. It was first used for car body design and manufacture in the early 1970s. Most schools have some form of CAM equipment, which can be used relatively easily.

Vinyl cutters

Vinyl cutters are common, and one of the more basic CAM machines. They are used to cut adhesive vinyl, and work in a similar way to a plotter. They are available in a variety of different sizes, from A4 upwards. Common uses in school are to create designs or logos to stick on to packaging or for creating lettering and images for vehicles.

The Roland CAMM1 and Stika are examples of vinyl cutters that you may have in school.

Figure 4.29 Vinyl cutters

Figure 4.28 Example of work produced using a vinyl cutter

Engravers

Engravers are usually small but extremely useful CAM machines, which can produce anything from lettering through to quite intricate graphics on a variety of different materials such as soft metals, wood, MDF and plastics. The same design can be reproduced in quantity, but this can take a long time depending on how complicated it is. Common uses in school are to create nameplates, logos, directional signs, machine components, promotional goods, raised lettering, PCB pattern engraving, etc. The Roland CAMM 2 and Vision Phoenix 1212 are examples of engravers that you may have in school.

Figure 4.30 Engravers

Figure 4.31 Examples of work using engraver

Laser cutters

Laser cutters are relatively new and not as common in schools as the other CAM machines that have been covered already. Laser cutting works by using a high-power laser, controlled by computer, to cut flat sheet material such as card, foam board, high-impact polystyrene sheet (HIPS) and acrylic. Depending on the type of material being cut, the material either melts, burns, vaporises or is blown away by a jet of gas.

Advantages of laser cutting over mechanical cutting are the high precision cutting it allows, and the lack of physical contact between the cutting edge and the material. This means it cannot get blocked – as there is no cutting blade that can become blocked by waste material. There is also a reduced chance of warping the material that is being cut, as laser systems have only a small heat-affected zone. Some materials are also very difficult, or even impossible, to cut by more traditional means.

One of the disadvantages of laser cutting is the high energy required.

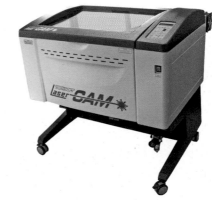

Figure 4.32 Laser cutter

Figure 4.33 Work produced using a laser cutter

Whatever CAD/CAM equipment you have access to, it is important to think of it as a 'tool' in the same way as a craft knife, cutting mat or any other tool. It has a place in the designing and making process and should be used appropriately, as and when it is needed. CAD/CAM should be used in conjunction with traditional 'hand skills' to enhance your work and demonstrate that you have, and can combine, a range of different skills.

KEY POINTS

- CAD/CAM should be used as a 'tool'.
- CAD/CAM is an ideal way to produce items in quantity.

EXAMINER'S TIPS

- Use CAD/CAM to enhance your design work and making work.
- Use CAD/CAM appropriately in conjunction with traditional 'hand skills'.

KEY TERMS

CAM – computer-aided manufacture
ENGRAVER – CAM machine for cutting and engraving MDF, acrylic and soft metals
LASER CUTTER – CAM machine for high-precision cutting of almost any material
VINYL CUTTER – CAM machine for cutting and scoring vinyl, paper, card, etc.

4.6 COMPUTER NUMERICAL CONTROL (CNC) MACHINES

LEARNING OUTCOME

By the end of this section you should have developed a knowledge and understanding of:

- how you can use CNC machines to enhance your making work.

CNC machines are computer-controlled machines that can cut and shape all sorts of different materials. The designs are loaded on to the computer, which then converts them into programs with instructions called G-Code. The code drives and controls a machine tool, which shapes and manufactures items by gradually removing material. The accuracy of the machine means that the final product is made to extremely high precision.

Figure 4.34 A Boxford CNC milling machine

Types of CNC machine

There are many different kinds of **CNC** machine available. In industry, very large and expensive CNC machines are used, but in school it is likely that you will have a relatively small CNC machine, such as a Boxford or Denford milling or routing machine.

CNC machines are designed for the shaping of resistant materials. In graphics their main use is to form and shape **Styrofoam**™ or **expanded polystyrene** as part of a graphic product, or to shape **MDF**, **Jelutong** or balsa wood to create moulds for vacuum forming using **HIPS**.

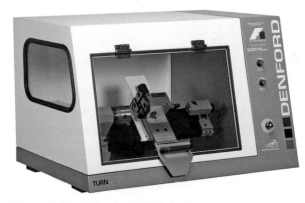

Figure 4.35 A Denford CNC lathe

Figure 4.36 Styrofoam™ point-of-sale display

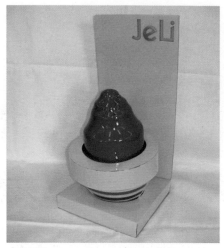

Figure 4.37 Vacuum-formed graphic product

In industry, due to the complexity of the products and machines used, it takes skilled operators to program and run CNC machines.

In school it is relatively easy to create a simple design for a mould or Styrofoam™ shape and transfer this to a CNC machine to produce.

The advantages of using the CNC machine in school are that:

- you can produce extremely accurate and high-quality products

Figure 4.38 Examples of Styrofoam™ moulds made using a CNC miller

- you can reproduce identical items time after time
- you can manufacture products in less time than it would take to do so by hand.

KEY POINTS

- CNC machines can be used to shape Styrofoam™ graphic products.
- CNC machines can be used to make vacuum-forming moulds.

EXAMINER'S TIP

Use CNC as a tool to enhance the making of your product.

KEY TERMS

CNC – computer numerical control
HIPS – high-impact polystyrene sheet
MDF – medium-density fibreboard
JELUTONG – a low-density, straight-grained hardwood, similar to balsa wood
STYROFOAM™ – polystyrene thermal insulation, blue or pink in colour and denser than expanded polystyrene
EXPANDED POLYSTYRENE – polystyrene foam, typically white and made of expanded polystyrene beads

CHAPTER 5

INDUSTRIAL PRODUCTION

5.1 COMMERCIAL PRODUCTION METHODS

By the end of this section you should have developed a knowledge and understanding of:

- one-off production
- quantity production
- rapid prototyping.

Methods of production can change depending on the type of product being made and the number of products required. Some production methods are very labour-intensive while others are almost fully automated.

Figure 5.1 Architectural model

One-off production

This is sometimes referred to as 'job', or 'jobbing', production.

One-off production involves the making of a single product, which is usually fully completed before the next one is started.

Because each product is individually made it can be a very labour-intensive and expensive method of production.

An architectural model, like the one shown in Figure 5.1, is a good example of a one-off product.

KEY POINTS

One-off production:

- is almost always produced to a specific client's requirements
- requires high skill levels
- usually involves low capital costs.

▶ Quantity production

Batch production

This method of production involves producing a specified number (a batch) of the same product. The numbers in a 'batch' can be large or small.

Batch production is a flexible system, which allows you to produce similar things but with variations. For example, one batch of wallpaper could be produced with a red design on it; a second batch could be produced that had the same design but printed in a different colour, as shown in Figure 5.2.

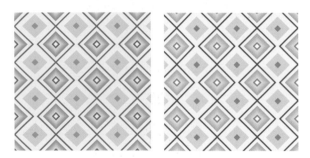

Figure 5.2 Batches of wallpaper printed in different colours

Newspapers are printed in batches. This allows for changes to be made, particularly to the front page, from an early morning edition to one produced later.

In a school situation you can use equipment such as laser cutters, photocopiers, cutter-plotters and computer printers as aids to producing small batches of the same product. Stencils, templates, jigs and formers can also help to maintain consistent results when batch-producing products.

KEY POINTS

Batch production:

- is a flexible system, allowing a wide range of different products to be produced
- can react to demand by stopping or increasing a production run
- requires a less skilled workforce than one-off production.

High-volume production

This is sometimes referred to as mass production. It involves producing large numbers of identical products. In fact, many high-volume production systems run for days, sometimes weeks, without stopping. Generally the system is fully automated and requires only a small workforce to maintain the process. While this type of production system is very expensive to set up, the unit cost is relatively low. Enforced stoppages can be very costly.

Plastic bottles, like the ones shown in Figure 5.3, are produced using high-volume production methods.

Figure 5.3 Plastic bottles

KEY POINTS

High volume production:

- does not allow any variations in a product
- requires regular high demand for a product in order to be economically viable
- involves high set up costs, but results in low unit costs
- requires a low-skilled workforce and involves high levels of automation.

EXAMINER'S TIPS

You should be able to name and briefly describe the various production methods. Support your answers by giving examples of products made by the method you have described. Always justify the reasons for your choice.

(a) Do an internet search and collect at least five images of products produced using each of the production methods that you need to be familiar with.

(b) Using a sheet of A3 paper for each production method, identify the products, what they are made from, who uses them, how much they cost and why you think that particular production method was chosen. Remember: you must justify the reasons you give.

Rapid prototyping

A rapid prototyping machine is used to fabricate three-dimensional objects directly from a CAD data source. It adds and bonds layers of material together to form objects, as shown in Figure 5.4.

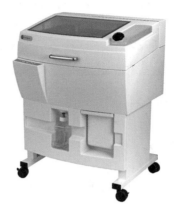

Built up layers of material

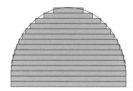

Figure 5.4 Rapid prototyping

This process is called additive fabrication. With additive fabrication the machine reads the data from a CAD drawing and lays down successive layers of either liquid, powder or sheet material, and in this way builds up the object from a series of cross-sections. The machine automatically joins the layers together to create the final shape.

One of the real benefits of rapid prototyping is that it dramatically reduces the amount of 'lead time' of products. This is the amount of time from a design being conceived until it is put into manufacture.

ACTIVITY

You can do a simulation of rapid prototyping by cutting out individual sections through a product, either by hand or using a laser cutter, and then gluing the sections together. The closer each section is in shape and size to the previous one the better the final profile will be. Start with a simple shape and build up to more complicated examples.

5.2 SUSTAINABILITY AND ENVIRONMENTAL ISSUES

LEARNING OUTCOMES

By the end of this section you should have developed a knowledge and understanding of:

- energy sources – finite and renewable
- sustainability
- environmental, social and economic issues
- the recycling of graphic materials
- the '6Rs'
- design for disassembly
- the concept of limited product lifetime
- why products are packaged
- globalisation.

Increasingly the design and manufacture of products is being influenced by environmental and sustainability issues. Many designers and manufacturers are addressing these issues, producing more products that are both socially responsible and environmentally friendly, as well as offering value for money.

▌ Energy sources

Currently, fossil fuels – mainly coal, oil and natural gas – are being used to produce 85% of the energy used globally. These types of energy source are **finite** – this means they will eventually run out.

Fossil fuels are generally converted into more useable forms of energy such as electricity, which, in the UK, is the main source of power for both industrial and domestic use.

The burning of fossil fuels has significant adverse effects on the **environment** because carbon dioxide (CO_2) is produced, which contributes to global warming.

Renewable energy sources are increasingly being used to produce power in ways that are both more environmentally friendly and sustainable. Renewable energy sources include hydro-electric, wind, solar, wave, geothermal and biomass.

Sustainability

The aim of sustainable design is to produce products and services in a way that reduces the use of non-renewable resources, minimises environmental impact and relates people to their natural environment.

EXAMINER'S TIP

When using materials and processes you should be aware of their effect on society and the environment in terms of sustainability, pollution, waste and 'recyclability'.

Principles of sustainable design

- Low-impact materials: choose non-toxic, sustainably produced or recycled materials that require little energy to process.

- Energy efficiency: use manufacturing processes and make products that require less energy.

- Quality and durability: longer-lasting and better-functioning products will not have to be replaced so often, thus reducing the impacts caused by producing replacements.

- Design for reuse and recycling: products

should be designed for performance in a 'commercial afterlife'.

Sustainable graphic design

Sustainable graphic design needs to consider the environmental impacts of products such as packaging, printed materials and publications, throughout a life cycle that includes: raw materials, **transformation**, manufacturing, transportation, use and disposal.

When subjecting a design to a sustainability audit a designer might consider:

- reducing the amount of materials required for production

- using paper and other materials that have been, or can be, recycled; printing with low-VOC (volatile organic compounds) inks

- using production and distribution methods that require the least amount of energy and transport

- whether the end product could be replaced by a digital, rather than printed, image

- whether the product could fulfil more than one purpose – for example, the design shown in Figure 5.5 is for a box to hold breakfast cereal; when the box has been emptied it can be used as a child's toy.

Figure 5.5 Cereal box

As a designer you need to be innovative when it comes to reducing, reusing and recycling. Taking items with former lives and reinventing them can produce unique and charming products as well as being environmentally responsible.

◗ The recycling of graphic materials

When we recycle, used materials are converted into new products, reducing the need to consume natural resources.

Most of the materials that are used to make graphic products can be recycled.

Paper

The main types of paper used every day that can be recycled are:

- newspapers, magazines, telephone directories and unwanted mail
- office paper
- packaging paper
- mixed or coloured paper.

Paper is made from cellulose fibres that are originally created from wood pulp. To reverse this process for the purpose of recycling the paper is soaked and agitated; it can then be pulped and reprocessed to make new products.

The process of recycling paper and cardboard can be repeated at least five times before the fibres eventually shorten and then disintegrate.

Nowadays the process of removing ink from paper only very occasionally involves the use of chemicals such as bleach. When the ink is not removed it results in the recycled paper having a greyish tinge.

In recent times the cost of recycled paper has gone down, while its quality continues to improve.

Recycled paper is commonly used in the production of:

- newspapers and magazines
- printing paper
- some types of cardboard.

Cardboard

Most cardboard can be recycled but it should not be mixed with other forms of paper like newspapers and magazines. Cardboard that has been in direct contact with food, such as the pizza box shown in Figure 5.6, is more difficult to recycle as it can contaminate the other cardboard.

Figure 5.6 Used pizza box

Corrugated cardboard is considered to be one of the easiest and most viable materials to recycle but it must not be mixed with other types of paper or board.

The processes involved in recycling cardboard are the same as for paper.

Some types of recycled paper-based materials should not be used in situations where they come directly into contact with food. There is a possibility that the food could be contaminated or tainted. For example, the outer packaging of the cereal box shown in Figure 5.7 has been made from recycled materials but virgin (new) material has been used to make the inner packaging.

Figure 5.7 Outer and inner packaging for cereals

Plastics

Plastics can be recycled but the process is more difficult because of the wide variety of different types of plastics used in the packaging industry. Although labelling does exist it can still be hard to identify specific types of plastic. Plastic also has a high volume-to-weight ratio, which can make recycling collections of plastic packaging waste less cost-effective than the collection of other recyclables that weigh more and take up less space.

Recycled plastic is used in the manufacture of products such as:

- flowerpots and containers
- fibres
- new packaging materials.

Mixed materials

Combining two or more materials to make a product makes recycling very difficult. Currently there are few recycling facilities that can deal with this type of product.

An example of a product made from several materials is the Tetra Pak shown in Figure 5.8, which consists of 75% paper, 20% polyethylene and 5% aluminium foil.

Figure 5.8 Tetra Pak

 EXAMINER'S TIP

The recyclability of products is a key issue that you can expect to feature in examination questions. Questions could ask you if a particular product was suitable for recycling or if its disposal would cause pollution or other damage to the environment.

The 6Rs

The '6Rs' (Recycle, Reuse, Reduce, Refuse, Rethink, Repair) provide a framework you can use to check that you are considering appropriate environmental, **social** and economic issues when you are designing and making products.

Recycle

- Can the materials I am using be recycled?
- Can I use recycled materials to make the product?

- Can the product be disassembled so that materials can be reprocessed for use in new products?

Reuse

- Can the product be reused for either the same or a new purpose?
- How could the product be adapted to suit an alternative use?

Reduce

- What will the life cycle of the product be?
- What will its **eco** footprint be like?
- Will it have built-in **obsolescence**?
- Will it waste energy and be a waste of the production process?
- Will materials be wasted?
- Could I use fewer materials but still produce a workable design?

Refuse

- Should I refuse to use certain materials?
- What issues related to sustainable design should I consider?

Rethink

- How is it possible for me to approach design problems differently?
- How can I make the design do the job better?

Repair

- Which parts of the product can/cannot be repaired?
- What parts of the design do I think might break and need replacing?
- How easy will it be to replace parts?

▌ Design for disassembly

Many designers and manufacturers are making a big effort to reduce the impact of their products on the environment. At the design stage, designers are considering how the product will be recycled at the end of its life.

One of the major difficulties with recycling happens when different materials are permanently joined together. For example, the packaging shown in Figure 5.9 has been made mainly from card, but a clear plastic window has been added so that the product inside can be seen. This combination of materials makes the packaging more difficult to recycle.

Figure 5.9 Packaging with a clear plastic window

Although most products can be disassembled eventually, lengthy **disassembly** does not make for economic recycling. This is because the cost of disassembly is likely to be higher than the money gained through recycling the materials from the product. It is for this reason that designing products for disassembly has increased in popularity. Designers are now producing products that are fixed together in semi-permanent ways so that the product can be disassembled at the end of its useful life and the individual parts reused or recycled easily.

Limited product lifetime

Many graphic products are designed to have only a limited lifetime.

Some, like the takeaway drink and food containers shown in Figure 5.10, are considered disposable. This means they are intended to be used only once and then disposed of – they are thrown away.

Figure 5.10 Disposable food and drink containers

Other items, like the film and music display stands and advertising material shown in Figure 5.11, are used only during a period of a

Figure 5.11 Promotional material for films and music

few weeks, or perhaps months, while the film or music is new and relevant to potential customers. Some of this type of material does, however, have a 'second life' because it becomes 'collectable'.

Graphic products, such as books and magazines, can be reused and read by a large number of people before they are finally thrown away.

Some products have what is called 'built-in (or planned) obsolescence'. This is the process of a product becoming obsolete, out of style and/or non-functional after a certain period or amount of use, in a way that is planned by the manufacturer. While this can increase demand for a company's product because consumers have to keep coming back again and again, it may work against the company because people go elsewhere to look for better-quality, longer-lasting products.

Effective recycling and reusing schemes can help to resolve some of the issues caused by a 'throwaway society'.

For example, the secondary packaging used to transport products from manufacturer to retail outlet is generally collected for recycling. But did you know that, in less than ten days, it can be on the shelves as new packaging?

In some cases, might it be better if some of this secondary packaging was reused rather than recycled?

Why products are packaged

Packaging has a fundamental role to play in the way brands communicate their image, values and the quality of their products (see Figure 5.12).

Figure 5.13 Primary packaging

Figure 5.12 A brand image

Packaging is an important part of any marketing strategy. The shapes, colours and images used can attract potential customers and encourage them to buy the product.

There are two main categories of packaging: primary and secondary.

Primary packaging

This is the packaging that appears on the shelf in the shop, as shown in Figure 5.13. It holds and displays the product.

Secondary packaging

This is the packaging used to store and transport the product, as shown in Figure 5.14. Each secondary packaging container holds and protects a number of primary packaged products.

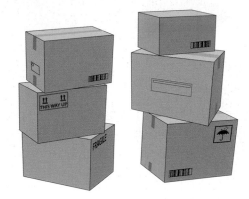

Figure 5.14 Secondary packaging

The main reasons that products are packaged are:

- for protection and, in the case of some food products, to increase their shelf life (see Figure 5.15)

Figure 5.15 Packaging to prolong the life of a product

Figure 5.17 Packaged goods on display

- for ease of transportation (secondary packaging), as shown in Figure 5.14

- for security – seals and tags make it harder to tamper with the packaging's contents, as shown in Figure 5.16

- to give the consumer information, as shown in Figure 5.18

- to create the right image and enable customers to identify the product easily – for example, plastic milk bottles all come in basically the same shape.

Figure 5.16 Security tags and seals

- for storage and display, as shown in Figure 5.17

EXAMINER'S TIP

You need to be able to give examples of how packaging is used to protect, transport, store, secure, display and give information about a product.

As manufacturers find ways of using fewer materials to make effective packaging, the amount of waste resulting from used packaging is reduced.

For example, a quick and easy solution to reducing packaging is the Co-op's Tomato Puree product. By removing the cardboard box that the tube used to be packaged in and placing the tubes upright, directly into the display packaging shown in Figure 5.19, the amount of packaging used has been reduced by over a third.

Lower in sugar cream filled éclairs		
Typical value	Per 100g	Per serving
Energy	1695 KJ 405 kcal	559 KJ 125 kcal
Protein	5.97 g	1.97 g
Carbohydrate of which sugars	18.4 g 5.18 g	6.07 g 1.52 g
Fat of which saturates	34.6 g 16.4 g	11.4 g 5.41 g
Fibre (NSP)	0.56 g	0.19 g
Sodium	0.27 g	0.09 g

Nutrition information – pizza		
	Typical values	
	per 100g	per serving 32 g
Energy	1168 kJ 279 kcal	374 kJ 89.3 kcal
Protein	12 g	3.84 g
Carbohydrate	49.2 g	15.7 g
Fat	5.16 g	1.65 g

Figure 5.18 Product information

Figure 5.19 Example of reduced packaging

 EXAMINER'S TIP

Exam questions could ask you to suggest ways in which the amount of material used for an existing piece of packaging could be reduced.

▶ Globalisation

One definition of globalisation is that it is 'a process of interaction among the people, companies and governments of different nations, a process driven by international trade and investment and added to by information technology'.

Globalisation has effects on the environment, on culture, on political systems, on economic development and prosperity, and on physical well-being in societies around the world.

As the number of global brands, such as McDonald's, Microsoft, Coca-Cola and Nike, continues to increase, we need to be aware of both the benefits and potential dangers of globalisation.

Some of the benefits of globalisation include:

- making a wider range of products available to a larger number of people
- increasing the market and/or demand for products
- increasing the free flow of trade between countries
- being able to take the best from different cultures and learn from the indigenous people of other countries
- being able to move ideas and information around the world easily and quickly via the internet, email and other global communication systems
- encouraging equality among different cultures
- better interaction between a greater number of people

- not having to have all of a company's expertise and facilities based in one location – a design could be created in one country, parts made in several different countries and the product assembled elsewhere; the downside of this is, of course, increased air miles.

The potential dangers of globalisation include:

- balancing the need for profits against the well-being of workers, customers and their environment
- it can result in locally produced sustainable design being replaced with mass-manufactured, polluting alternatives – for example, drinking mugs made from locally sourced materials being replaced with disposable plastic cups
- designers and manufacturers not being aware of local practices and alternatives before starting a new design
- imposing one preconceived way of thinking/acting/doing things on any given society
- not taking into account the possible need for products to be customised to meet the requirements of a particular region
- standardisation reducing variation in types of product.

When large organisations manufacture items to satisfy a global market this must not result in weak compromises but should produce inspiring, innovative products that are both socially responsible and environmentally friendly, as well as offering value for money.

EXAMINER'S TIP

Take great care not to produce graphic images or products that could in any way offend the attitudes, values and beliefs of various cultures and minority groups of people.

ACTIVITY

(a) In your class group, identify a range of environment issues that you are concerned about. These could be local issues – such as the litter problem in your school or trying to reduce the amount of energy that you use at home – or more wide-ranging ones, such as global warming.

(b) After a group discussion, individually identify an issue that you want to make people more aware of.

(c) Identify a communication method that you will use for your awareness campaign. This could be a leaflet, a poster, a web page or any other method you feel appropriate.

(d) Using your chosen media, design an awareness campaign based on an environmental issue.

KEY TERMS

BIODEGRADABLE – a material that will break down (rot) over a period of time

DISASSEMBLY – taking an object apart

ECO – mostly used as a prefix to another word, such as eco-friendly, eco-label or eco-tourism, to suggest that a product is less damaging to the environment

ENVIRONMENT – everything around us, our surroundings, including the natural world and the made world

FINITE – materials or energy from sources that will run out and cannot be replaced

GLOBAL MANUFACTURING – modern-day industrial practice of designing in one part of the world and manufacturing in another where material and labour costs may be cheaper

OBSOLESCENCE – when products go out of use as they are replaced by better and/or more stylish products; some products are said to have 'built-in obsolescence' either for safety purposes or to ensure demand for new products

RENEWABLE – materials or energy produced from sources that can be replaced

SOCIAL – relating to groups of people

TRANSFORMATION – combining of raw materials to make a component or other material

CHAPTER 6

HEALTH AND SAFETY

6.1 DESIGNER RESPONSIBILITIES

By the end of this section you should have developed a knowledge and understanding of:

- a designer's duty of care
- what designers must do to ensure safety.

*Designers have a responsibility, or **duty**, to make sure that the products we use are safe. This is sometimes called a duty of care. This responsibility is only applicable if the product is used for the **purpose** for which it was intended, by the **users** it was intended for and in the **environment** it was intended for.*

Designer responsibilities and limits

Purpose

Many products have a primary **function** or purpose. For example, a pencil sharpener is meant to sharpen pencils. The designer has a responsibility to ensure that the pencil sharpener performs this function safely and without any risk to the user.

Some products are multi-functional or multi-purpose. For example, a polystyrene cup might have to hold both hot and cold liquids. The designer has a responsibility to ensure that the cup performs both of these functions without risk to the user.

Sometimes products are used for a purpose for which they are not intended. For example, a craft knife might be used as a screwdriver. The designer cannot be held responsible if a person is injured using a product for a purpose for which it was not intended.

Users

Many products are designed to be used by the majority of, or perhaps all, the population. For example, a pencil can be used by people of all ages.

Some products are designed to be used by a specific group of people. For example, a pop-up book might be designed for children aged between 5 and 7 years.

Sometimes products are used by people they

Figure 6.1 A pop-up book aimed at children

are not intended for. For example, a ride-on child's toy might be used by an adult. The designer cannot be held responsible if a person is injured using a product that is not intended for them.

Environment

Many products are designed to be used in a wide range of **environments** or surroundings. For example, a torch can be used inside and outside the home.

Some products are designed to be used in specific surroundings. For example, a waterproof watch might be designed to be used by swimmers.

Sometimes products are used in environments they are not intended for. For example, a safety sign printed on paper might be displayed outside. The designer cannot be held responsible if a user is injured because the weather has made the safety sign unreadable.

KEY POINT

Designers have a responsibility to take reasonable care to ensure that users are not injured by the product they have designed. This is called a duty of care. This responsibility is applicable only if the product is used for the purpose it was intended, by the users it was intended for and in the environment it was intended for.

EXAMINER'S TIP

Test questions may ask you to comment on what designers can do to make sure people are not injured by the products they have designed. You should comment on how they can make the purpose, users and environment for use clear in their instructions.

QUESTION

Consider the instructions for a range of electrical products: do they make the purpose, users and environment for use clear?

KEY TERMS

DUTY – what you have to do
ENVIRONMENT – surroundings
FUNCTION – purpose
USERS – people who use a product

6.2 PERSONAL SAFETY

By the end of this section you should have developed a knowledge and understanding of:

- steps to take to ensure your personal safety.

Personal safety is about making sure people are not exposed to unnecessary risk of harm. We all have a responsibility to make sure that we, and those around us, are safe.

Ensuring personal safety

The key considerations in ensuring **personal safety** are as follows.

Using personal protection equipment

You should always use any personal protection equipment that is provided for a specific situation. For example, eye protection should be worn when working on a sanding machine. Other types of personal protection are face masks, ear defenders, safety shoes and overalls.

Using tools and equipment safely

You should always make sure that tools and equipment are safe for use. For example, a chuck guard should be correctly fitted to a drilling machine. Other examples of tool and equipment safety are the installation of emergency stop buttons and the safe storage of tools.

Maintaining a safe environment

You should always check that the working environment is safe. For example, there should not be things left lying around that someone could trip over. Other ways of maintaining a safe environment are to have dust extraction systems and clearly marked walkways.

Accident procedures

Even though you may have taken steps to ensure your personal safety, and the safety of others, accidents will happen from time to time. It is, therefore, very important to understand the procedures to be followed in the case of an accident.

Figure 6.2 Personal protection equipment

While specific instructions may differ, the general **principles** are as follows:

1. Make the scene of the accident safe, so that no more injuries occur.
2. Assess the injury (summon assistance if required).
3. Treat the injury (either on-site or in hospital).
4. Write an accident report.
5. Undertake any work required to make sure the accident does not happen again.

QUESTIONS

1. List three things you can do to improve your personal safety.
2. State three things you would do after an accident has taken place.

KEY POINT

Personal safety is about making sure people are not **exposed** to unnecessary risk of harm. This involves using personal protection equipment, using tools and equipment safely, maintaining a safe environment and having accident procedures in place.

EXAMINER'S TIPS

Test questions may ask you to identify things that can be done to improve safety. Focus your answers on the key areas, such as using the personal protection equipment listed previously.

KEY TERMS

EXPOSED – out in the open
PERSONAL – belonging to an individual
PRINCIPLES – main things

6.3 RISK ASSESSMENT

LEARNING OUTCOMES

By the end of this section you should have developed a knowledge and understanding of:

- what is meant by risk assessment
- identifying a specific risk
- assessing the probability
- minimising the risk.

Risk assessment is about assessing, or measuring, how great the risk is of harm to someone. Almost everything we do carries some risk. For example, if you use a craft knife there is a risk you might cut yourself.

▶ Aspects of risk assessment

There are three aspects to risk assessment. They are as follows.

1. Identifying the **specific** risk: this means finding out exactly what the specific risk is. For example, using a vacuum-forming machine carries some risk that you might either burn yourself or get an electric shock. There is very little risk that you might cut yourself.

2. Assessing the **probability**: once you have identified the specific risk, you then need to assess the probability, or chances, of an accident happening. There are several ways that this can be done, but one of the best indicators is what has happened before. If, under the same circumstances, accidents have happened before, the risk might be considered unacceptably high. If, under the same circumstances, an accident has never happened before the risk might be considered very low and you would be happy to undertake the task.

3. **Minimising** the risk: once you have identified the specific risk and assessed the likelihood of an accident taking place, you must consider whether there is anything you can do to minimise, or reduce, the risk. For example, you will reduce the likelihood of an accident when using a vacuum-forming machine if you have had proper training on the use of the machinery. It is always wise to minimise any risks.

KEY POINT

Almost everything we do carries some risk. Risk assessment is concerned with identifying the specific risk, assessing the probability and then minimising the risk. After you have considered these three aspects the risk either becomes acceptable (a chance you are willing to take) or unacceptable (the risk of injury is too great).

EXAMINER'S TIP

Test questions will focus on your understanding of risk assessment and what can be done to reduce the chances of an injury occurring.

ACTIVITY

Carry out a risk assessment of a practical task using the following headings:

- Identifying the specific risk
- Assessing the probability
- Minimising the risk.

KEY TERMS

MINIMISING – reducing as much as is possible
PROBABILITY – chances of something happening
SPECIFIC – definite

6.4 COSHH

By the end of this section you should have developed a knowledge and understanding of:

- what is meant by COSHH
- an overview of the COSHH regulations.

Using chemicals or other hazardous substances can put people's health at risk, so the law requires employers to control exposure to hazardous substances. In order to do this, employers have to comply with the Control of Substances Hazardous to Health Regulations 2002 (COSHH).

An overview of the COSHH regulations

Hazardous substances include:

- **substances** generated during work activities (e.g. fumes from soldering and welding)
- naturally occurring substances (e.g. grain dust)
- biological agents such as bacteria and other micro-organisms
- substances used directly in work activities (e.g. adhesives or paints).

Examples of the effects of hazardous substances include:

- skin irritation or dermatitis as a result of skin contact

- asthma as a result of developing allergy to substances used
- losing consciousness as a result of being overcome by toxic fumes
- cancer, which may appear long after exposure to the chemical that caused it
- infection from bacteria and other micro-organisms (biological agents).

The positive benefits from carefully following through the requirements of COSHH are:

- improved productivity as a result of using more effective controls (e.g. reduced use of raw materials)
- improved **employee** morale
- better employee understanding and compliance with health and safety requirements.

KEY POINT

COSHH stands for the Control of Substances Hazardous to Health. The law requires **employers** to control exposure to hazardous substances in order to prevent ill health.

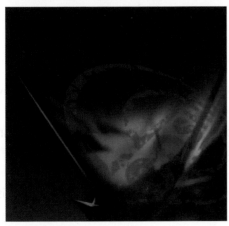

COSHH: A brief guide to the Regulations
What you need to know about the Control of Substances Hazardous to Health Regulations 2002 (COSHH)

Figure 6.3 COSHH regulations

EXAMINER'S TIP

Test questions will ask you what impact COSHH has on using and storing substances. Make sure you are able to give at least one example of each that relates to working with graphic materials.

KEY TERMS

EMPLOYEE – worker
EMPLOYER – someone who has workers
HAZARDOUS – dangerous
SUBSTANCE – material

6.5 SAFETY SYMBOLS

LEARNING OUTCOMES

By the end of this section you should have developed a knowledge and understanding of:

* the reasons for safety symbols
* some common safety symbols.

Symbols are pictures that convey a message with the minimum use of words. Safety symbols are commonly used in the workplace to indicate such things as that eye protection must be worn.

▶ Safety symbols

Safety symbols must be clear and easy to understand. **Geometrical shapes**, bold images and colour are used to convey the message. **Colour associations** – such as red for danger and green for go – are important aspects of **conveying** the message.

KEY POINT

Safety symbols convey a message with the minimum use of words.

Figure 6.4 Common safety symbols

ACTIVITY

Design a safety symbol to show that a gas tap must be turned off.

KEY TERMS

COLOUR ASSOCIATION – e.g. red for danger
CONVEY – put across or communicate
GEOMETRICAL SHAPES – square, circle or triangle

EXAMINER'S TIP

Make sure you are familiar with the safety symbols in Figure 6.4 and can state what they are designed to show. You should also be able to comment on how the designer has used shapes, images and colour to convey the message.

QUALITY

7.1 QUALITY OF DESIGN

By the end of this section you should have developed a knowledge and understanding of:

- what is meant by quality of design
- the features that define quality of design.

Quality of design is concerned with how well a product is designed. It has nothing to do with how well a product is made.

Features of a quality design

Users will have different views on what they consider to be a quality design. For example, some users will feel a product is a quality design because it looks nice. Others may consider a new way of doing something to be the mark of a quality design. This difference in views is understandable because there is an element of **user perception**, or user feelings, when making a judgement about the quality of a design.

While user views may differ, the common features that define quality of design do not. Quality designs must meet the following requirements.

Figure 7.1 Good or bad design?

Function as intended

The **functions** of a product are the things it is meant to do. In order to be considered a quality design, a product must fulfil its function as well as, or better than, expected. For example, you would expect a calendar to clearly show the days of each month of the year. If it did not, you would consider the design to be of poor quality.

Be aesthetically pleasing

Aesthetics is concerned with the look of a product. In order to be considered a quality design, a product must be pleasing to the eye. For example, one would expect a package for a chocolate bar to encourage people to buy the product. If it did not, it would not be a quality design. The two elements that contribute to the aesthetic qualities of a product are form and surface graphics. Form is the physical shape of the object. Surface graphics are the colour, lettering and images that are applied to the form.

Have user appeal

User appeal is concerned with how much people want or **desire** a product. In order to be a quality design, people must want to buy the product. This might not happen immediately: some designs are ahead of their time and it takes time for demand for the product to grow (Figure 7.2).

What makes something desirable is more difficult to define but it usually means it has an 'edge', or advantage, over its competitors. For example, a product might offer a new way of doing something, have more features or be available in a wide range of colours. In order to gain this 'edge', designers look at what is already available in the marketplace and then look to add something extra to make the product desirable.

Be sustainable

Sustainable designs will stand the test of time. This means that they will not have a negative impact on the environment, society and the economy during manufacture, use or disposal at the end of their useful life. For example, sustainable advertising might be made from recycled card, use little electricity for illumination and be easily disassembled for recycling at the end of its useful life.

Figure 7.3 Sustainable advertising?

Figure 7.2 Slow start, happy ending

KEY POINTS

There is an element of user perception in making judgements about the quality of a design, but all quality designs must:

- function as intended
- be aesthetically pleasing
- have user appeal
- be sustainable.

ACTIVITY

Analyse a range of existing products to develop your understanding of the four features that define quality of design.

1. State two functions of a point-of-sale display stand.
2. Name two ways of making a product more aesthetically pleasing.
3. Name two ways of making a product more sustainable.

KEY TERMS

AESTHETICS – the appearance of a product
DESIRE – to want a product
FUNCTION – what a product is meant to do
SUSTAINABLE – the ability to last for a period of time
USER PERCEPTION – user feelings based on the senses of sight, hearing, taste, touch and smell

7.2 QUALITY OF MANUFACTURE

LEARNING OUTCOMES

By the end of this section you should have developed a knowledge and understanding of:

- what is meant by quality of manufacture
- the features that define quality of manufacture.

Quality of manufacture is concerned with how well a product is made. It has nothing to do with how well it has been designed.

Features that define quality of manufacture

The main features that define quality of manufacture are as follows.

Appropriate material selection

Material **selection** is about choosing the correct material. A high quality of **manufacture** may not be achieved unless the material selection is appropriate for the

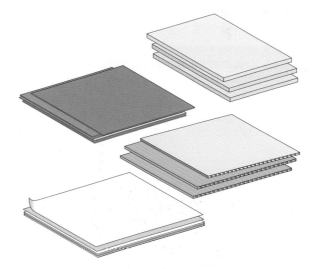

Figure 7.4 A range of materials

product – for example, it would be very difficult to make an aerosol can from foam board. Cost, availability, environmental issues and working properties are important considerations when selecting a material. (Chapter 2 looks at materials and the criteria for selecting materials in more detail.)

Appropriate manufacturing methods

Once a material has been chosen, appropriate manufacturing **methods** need to be selected to shape, join and finish the material. Inappropriate selections will almost certainly result in a poor quality of manufacture. For example, it would be unwise to select vacuum forming as a method of shaping corriflute. The **scale of production**, availability of equipment, energy use, and health and safety are important factors to be considered when selecting manufacturing methods.

High-quality surface finish

In many respects the surface finish is determined by the material selection and the manufacturing method. For example, the quality of a printed document is largely determined by the paper and the printer. However, this is not so in the case of an **applied finish**. For example, it is possible to select an appropriate material and manufacturing method but end up with an unsatisfactory surface finish – perhaps poorly applied paint. Many consumers consider the surface finish to be the most critical aspect in determining the quality of manufacture, so it is really worth making sure that this is as good as possible.

Appropriately fitting components

When a product is made from several **components**, the parts must fit together to the required degree of accuracy. This degree of accuracy is called tolerance and is explained later in this chapter. Remember, some components are meant to fit together without a gap, while others require a gap to allow the parts to move freely.

Production method	Example	Advantages	Disadvantages
One-off production	Model of a theatre set	Flexible – customer can have exactly what they want	Labour intensive
Batch production	Programme for a concert	Can easily be adapted for another batch. For example change the date or time of the concert	Requires templates, jigs or formers for cost-effective production
Quantity production (mass or continuous flow)	Cereal packaging	Low unit costs	High set up costs

Figure 7.5 Scales of production

KEY POINTS

The four main features that define quality of manufacture are:

1. appropriate material selection
2. appropriate manufacturing methods
3. high-quality surface finish
4. appropriately fitting components.

KEY TERMS

APPLIED FINISH – adding a 'coating' during or after manufacture
COMPONENT – part of a product
MANUFACTURE – the process of making
METHOD – a way of doing something
SCALE OF PRODUCTION – amount to be made (one-off, batch or mass)
SELECTION – choosing

ACTIVITY

Consider why products have not achieved a high quality of manufacture. List your answers under the following subheadings:

- Material selection
- Manufacturing methods
- Surface finish
- Component fit.

7.3 QUALITY PRODUCT

LEARNING OUTCOME

By the end of this section you should have developed a knowledge and understanding of:

- what is meant by a quality product.

A quality product brings together quality of design and quality of manufacture.

Figure 7.6 A quality product

▶ Features that define a quality product

The combination of quality of design and quality of manufacture does not always result in a quality product. For example, a product can be:

- a poor design that is made badly
- a poor design that is made well
- a good design that is made badly.

A product can only be a quality product if it is a good design that is made to a high standard. In order for this to happen, the features that define quality of design and quality of manufacture need to come together to ensure the product:

- functions as intended
- is aesthetically pleasing
- has user appeal
- is sustainable
- is made from appropriate materials
- is made by appropriate manufacturing methods

- has a good surface finish
- components fit together to the required degree of accuracy.

If any one of these features is missing the product cannot be considered a quality product.

KEY POINT

Remember that a quality product can be achieved only by successfully combining a good quality of design and a high quality of manufacture.

EXAMINER'S TIP

Make sure you develop a clear understanding of quality of design, quality of manufacture and a quality product.

◗ 7.4 TOLERANCE

LEARNING OUTCOMES

By the end of this section you should have developed a knowledge and understanding of:

- what is meant by the term tolerance
- acceptable working tolerances.

*The term tolerance refers to the level of accuracy to which something is made or drawn. In graphics this is often expressed as a plus or minus figure – how much above or below the **specified** measurement is acceptable.*

The term tolerance can also be applied to such things as weight, colour and temperature. The remainder of this section uses measurement to explain tolerance, but you should consider how other types of tolerance might be applied to products made in graphics.

Acceptable working tolerances

It is easy to believe that everything should be produced to a zero tolerance. This means that if a line is meant to be 100 mm long, the only acceptable length is 100 mm. However, this is not the case.

Figure 7.7 Tolerance

In graphics we usually work to a tolerance of plus or minus 2 mm. This means that a line of 100 mm in length is within tolerance (acceptable) if it is between 98 mm and 102 mm. In most cases this small **variation** will make no difference to the way the product functions. For example, if you are positioning a self-adhesive barcode on a package, the exact position is not critical: 2 mm either way will make no difference. However, there are cases where working to a tolerance of 2 mm would be unacceptable. For example, the colours in an inkjet printer must be aligned to a much smaller tolerance than 2 mm or the printed image will be unclear.

Figure 7.8 Acceptable working tolerances

The acceptable working tolerance for a product is determined by calculating the maximum variation (plus or minus) from the specified size that will allow the product to function as planned. A tolerance should not be smaller than that which is necessary for the product to function as intended as this may unnecessarily increase manufacturing costs.

KEY POINTS

Remember that:

- most products are manufactured to a tolerance

- an acceptable working tolerance is determined by calculating the maximum variation (plus or minus) that will allow the product to function as intended

- a tolerance traditionally refers to size, but can also be applied to such things as weight, colour and temperature.

EXAMINER'S TIPS

Consider a range of products and the tolerances to which they have been produced. A typical examination question might ask you to state and justify a tolerance for a specific product.

KEY TERMS

SPECIFIED – given or stated
VARIATION – difference from that specified

7.5 QUALITY CONTROL

LEARNING OUTCOMES

By the end of this section you should have developed a knowledge and understanding of:

- what is meant by quality control
- some types of quality control checks
- marks and symbols that inform consumers about quality.

*Quality control is about ensuring that products **conform** to standards that will ensure they are safe to use.*

▶ Aspects of quality control

The two main aspects of quality control are:

- quality control checks
- quality marks and symbols.

Quality control checks

Quality control checks are required to ensure that a product is manufactured to the specified standards. This will involve:

- identifying key quality control points in the manufacturing process
- selecting appropriate quality control checks
- establishing tolerances for the quality control checks.

For example, one quality control point in the production of a wedding invitation might come after the printing of the first draft copy. The quality control check might be that the customer visually checks the design. The tolerances might be plus or minus 5 mm in terms of positioning of the text, and zero in terms of spelling and grammar. In other

words, the positioning of the text must be within 5 mm of the specified position and all the text must be correctly spelt.

Figure 7.9 Customer visually checking a wedding invitation

Many other quality control checks, such as weighing, colour accuracy or temperature variation, are used in industry. These are often undertaken by computer-controlled technology, which largely removes the possibility of human error. In high-volume production, manufacturers may undertake quality control checks on perhaps 1 in every 1000 products. From the results of these 'spot checks' they will draw conclusions about the quality of the entire production run.

Figure 7.10 High-volume production

If a quality control check identifies that an aspect of a product – perhaps the position of a hole – is outside tolerance the problem should be **rectified** quickly as it is costly to produce lots of faulty products that cannot be sold. Appropriate action might include adjusting a machine setting or fitting a new part.

Quality marks and symbols

Quality marks and **symbols** are used to inform the customer that the product has been manufactured to an agreed standard and is safe to use. The most commonly used marks and symbols are described below.

ISO 9000

ISO 9000 is one of the most well-known families of standards among more than 17,400 published by the International Organization for Standardization (ISO) for business, government and society. The ISO 9000 family is for quality management and includes ISO 9001, which gives the requirements for a quality management system to ensure continual improvement of the organization's processes and customer

satisfaction. The ISO 9000 standards are used in manufacturing and services, in both public and private sectors, and apply to business processes relating to products, services, processed materials, hardware and software.

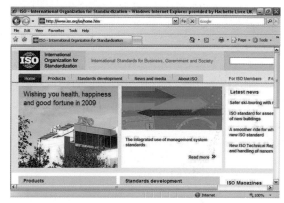

Figure 7.11 International Organization for Standardization

British Standard Kitemark

A Kitemark means the British Standards Institute (BSI) has independently tested a product, confirmed that the product conforms to the relevant British Standard, and has issued a licence to the company to use the Kitemark. The manufacturer pays for this service. The Kitemark is the symbol that gives consumers the assurance that the product they have bought really does

Figure 7.12 Kitemark

conform to the appropriate British Standard and should therefore be safe and reliable. Manufacturers are not legally required to display a Kitemark on their products, but many everyday products and appliances, such as fridges, electrical plugs and crash helmets, have them.

CE mark

The CE mark is used on many products sold in the European Economic Area (EEA). The CE mark certifies that a product has met European Union health, safety and environmental requirements, which ensure consumer safety. Many products, such as new toys, must meet this legal requirement before they can be sold within the European Community. Some products carry both a Kitemark and CE mark.

Figure 7.13 CE mark

Copyright mark

Copyright protects creative or artistic works. You can copy or use a copyrighted work only with the copyright owner's permission. You can copyright:

- instruction manuals, computer programs and song lyrics
- photographs, technical drawings, diagrams and logos
- layouts used to publish work.

Copyright applies to any medium. This means that you must not reproduce copyright-protected work in another medium without permission. This includes publishing photographs on the internet, making a sound recording of a book, and so on. A copyright-protected work can have more than one copyright. For example, an album of music can have separate copyrights for individual songs, sound recordings and artwork.

Figure 7.14 Copyright symbol

Trademark (trades and services mark)

A trademark protects any sign or symbol that allows a customer to tell a company or business apart from its competitors. You can register a name, logo, slogan, shape, colour or sound. A trademark must be:

- distinctive for the goods and services you provide
- not deceptive, or contrary to law or morality.

A registered trademark must be renewed every ten years to keep it in force.

Figure 7.15 A common trademark

The 'e' mark

The 'e' mark is used on a label to indicate that a product has been packed according to the requirements of the European Communities' average weight rules. Products with contents of 5 grams or greater must state the weight, preceded by the 'e' mark on the packaging. Products with contents less than 5 grams do not require the 'e' mark.

Figure 7.16 'e' mark

KEY POINTS

Quality control is concerned with:

- checking that a product is manufactured to the correct standards
- informing the consumer that the product has been manufactured to agreed standards.

EXAMINER'S TIPS

You may be asked to explain how the quality of a product is guaranteed – this refers to quality control. You may also be asked to explain how the quality standards are communicated to the consumer – this refers to quality marks and symbols.

KEY TERMS

CONFORM – to fall into line with
RECTIFIED – put right
SYMBOL – pictures that represent ideas or concepts

CHAPTER 8

UNIT A531: INTRODUCTION TO DESIGN AND MAKING

8.1 AN OVERVIEW OF UNIT A531: INTRODUCTION TO DESIGN AND MAKING

LEARNING OUTCOMES

By the end of this section you should have developed a knowledge and understanding of:

- how this unit fits into your qualification
- how the unit is assessed.

*Unit A531: Introduction to Design and Making is one of four **units** that you will need to study to gain a GCSE qualification in Design and Technology: Graphics. If you study the GCSE short course you will need to study this Unit and Unit A532.*

▶ Overview

Assessment of this unit is through a 20-hour controlled assessment. The assessment can be taken in January and June. You are allowed to take the assessment twice, with the highest score counting towards your **qualification**. Your teacher will help you decide if you are ready to undertake the work for this unit.

You are required to **research**, **design** and **make** a functioning prototype product.

You must select one of the **themes** that are published by OCR as a starting point for the task. The themes are reviewed periodically. Your teacher will be able to give you the current list of OCR published themes.

Your school is allowed to contextualise the theme and the starting point appropriately to reflect its own or community resources, and access to local business and industry that may add realism to your work. The task can be linked to your interests or other influences such as competitions, commerce or the community. You are not allowed to use the same theme for this unit as submitted or intended for submission for Unit A533.

Theme	Starting Point
PROMOTIONAL ITEMS	A freebie/give-away item that could be a calendar, pop-up mailers, direct mail, stamps to promote a significant event, concert/theatre promotion.
CORPORATE/BRAND IDENTITY	A range of items that could include company/brand logo, business cards, letterheads, company livery, promotional items, uniforms, menus, corporate gifts, bags.
SIGNS & DISPLAY	Situations could include exhibitions, estate agents, retail stores, sporting events, museums, libraries, temporary direction signs and information signs.
VISUAL COMMUNICATION	Wordless signs that can be understood in any language/culture, visual instructions for emergency situations (e.g. in the event of fire), children's party invitations, a range of greeting cards.
TRAVEL & TOURISM	Airline promotion (tickets, baggage, brochure, emergency situation instructions etc.), travel company direct mail, visitor centre information, theme park/underground train maps.
RETAIL ENVIRONMENT	Game/CD/DVD sleeve/inserts, Fairtrade in-store promotion/product. Mobile phone/iPod/MP3 promotion.
FOOD & DRINK	Product that can be flat packed, including fast food/convenience packaging, wrap around labels, cartons, drink/food carrier, disposable cup sleeve.
EDUCATION	Visual aid(s) for primary school children to teach them about recycling, teaching aid(s) to develop language skills.

Table 8.1 Unit A531 controlled assessment themes for 2010

Aims of this assessment

This unit aims to assess your ability to:

- demonstrate creativity
- demonstrate designing skills
- demonstrate good making skills
- demonstrate critical evaluation skills.

You will be required to produce:

- a number of concise worksheets or design presentation boards (A3, A4 or digital equivalent), showing design development and **modelling**, which may include the use of ICT to support the design process

- a prototype product – capable of evaluation
- a minimum of two digital photographs of your prototype, showing the front and back views of the product in use
- digital images/photographs of any models/mock-ups used when designing, modelling or testing
- a completed OCR cover sheet.

Submission of controlled assessment work

Your **controlled assessment** work can be submitted on paper or in electronic format but not a mixture of the two.

Work submitted on paper

A 'Contents' page with a numbering system should be included to aid organisation. All your work should be on the same-size paper but it does not matter what size paper you use. You can produce your work by hand or using ICT.

Work submitted electronically

Your work will need to be organised in folders so that the evidence can be accessed easily by a teacher or moderator. This structure is commonly known as a folder tree. There should be a top-level folder detailing your centre number, candidate number, surname and forename, together with the unit code A531. The next folder down should be called 'Home Page', which will be an index of all your work. The evidence for each section of the work should then be contained in a separate folder, containing appropriately named files. These files can be from the Microsoft Office suite, Movie, Audio, Graphics, Animation, Structured Mark-up or Text formats. PowerPoint is an ideal platform for producing electronic portfolios.

EXAMINER'S TIPS

- Prepare for the assessment by looking back over past design and make tasks.
- Check with your teacher well in advance of the assessment dates to see what you need to do in order to be ready to take the assessment.
- Plan how you will use the time available for the assessment task.
- Always explain your ideas thoroughly and concisely. Do not assume the reader has any knowledge of what you are doing.

KEY TERMS

CONTROLLED ASSESSMENT – work done under controlled conditions, authenticated as the student's own work

DESIGN – to plan something

EXTERNALLY MODERATED – sent to OCR for standardisation of marks

MODELLING – models that help test an idea

PROTOTYPE PRODUCT – the first example of a product that could be further developed or modified

QUALIFICATION – a GCSE or GCSE short course

THEME – starting point of the task

UNIT – part of a qualification

KEY POINTS

Unit A531: Introduction to Design and Making is:

- one of four units required for a GCSE in Design and Technology: Graphics
- assessed through a 20-hour controlled assessment available in January and June
- marked by your teachers and **externally moderated** by OCR examiners.

8.2 WHAT DO I NEED TO DO FOR THIS UNIT?

By the end of this section you should have developed a knowledge and understanding of:

- the task you are required to undertake
- how to choose a theme
- what is an 'acceptable' graphic outcome.

The task that you undertake for this unit requires you to:

- *select a theme*
- *identify a product/starting point*
- *carry out research*
- *produce a design*
- *make a prototype*
- *evaluate the process.*

Selecting a theme

To be successful in this unit you should choose a theme that:

- you can identify a product or starting point for
- best suits your capabilities and interests
- best suits the resources of your school/college
- brings out the best of your ability.

Graphic materials	Paper Card and board Foam board Sheet plastic – up to 1 mm thick Rigid foam
Joining materials	PVA adhesive, spray adhesive, solvent cement, hot melt glue (glue gun), epoxy resin, glue sticks, single and double sided tape, Velcro, double sided sticky pads, paper fasteners, eyelets, press fit 'click' fasteners, Clic rivets (plastic rivets)
Smart and modern materials	Polymorph, thermochromic inks, pigments and film, photochromic inks and pigments, phosphorent pigments, fluorescent pigments, other 'Smart' and modern materials as they become available
Pre-manufactured components	Staples, press fasteners, plastic rivets, plastic nuts and bolts.

Table 8.2 Compliant materials for Unit A531

▶ Graphic product outcomes

Graphic outcomes may be either two- or three-dimensional products that must be made from compliant materials. Compliant materials must be able to be shaped, folded, cut and joined. The compliant materials for this unit are paper, card/board, foam board, thin sheet plastic, rigid foam, smart materials and appropriate pre-manufactured components.

▶ Assessment strands

You will be required to provide evidence for four separate assessment strands in this unit, as detailed below.

Strand 1: Demonstrate Creativity

- Use appropriate recording and drawing techniques, including the use of **ICT**.
- Identify the principles of good design and relate products to the needs of users.
- Identify the significance of trends in existing products.

Strand 2: Demonstrate Designing Skills

- Produce an appropriate and considered response to a design brief.
- Produce a detailed **specification** for the product.
- Use detailed notes and annotated drawings to record original design ideas.
- Use a range of graphic skills and techniques.
- Use **CAD** to support design development.
- Clearly communicate details of the chosen design for prototype production.

Strand 3: Demonstrate Good Making Skills

- Make reasoned decisions about materials/components.
- Use appropriate making or trialling techniques to aid product development.
- Select appropriate equipment.
- Work skilfully and safely to produce a high-quality prototype that is fit for purpose.
- Demonstrate ability to produce surface graphics to a high level of competency.
- Apply knowledge of **digital media** and new technologies as appropriate.
- Demonstrate a practical and thorough understanding and ability in solving technical problems effectively and efficiently as they arise.
- Record the key stages in the making of the prototype product.

Strand 4: Demonstrate Critical Evaluation Skills

- Evaluate the processes involved in making the final product/prototype.
- Reflect on the evaluation and suggest modifications to improve the prototype product.

KEY POINTS

- There are four strands to this unit: Demonstrate Creativity, Demonstrate Designing Skills, Demonstrate Good Making Skills and Demonstrate Critical Evaluation Skills. Your work should address each of these strands.
- Your graphic outcome may be either two- or three-dimensional.
- Your graphic outcome must be made from the compliant materials outlined in the **course specification**.

EXAMINER'S TIPS

- Keep an open mind at the start of the task.
- Organise your activity; use time effectively.
- The four strands form the basis of the task – do not leave any of them out.

QUESTIONS

1. In what four key strands does this unit assess you?
2. What are you required to produce for this unit?

KEY TERMS

CAD – computer-aided design
CAM – computer-aided manufacture
COURSE SPECIFICATION – the OCR booklet that outlines GCSE Design and Technology: Graphics
DIGITAL MEDIA – cameras, scanners, sound recording
EVALUATION – asking how well the making process went
GRAPHIC OUTCOME – what you will make
ICT – information and communication technology
SPECIFICATION – the requirements of your chosen product
SURFACE GRAPHICS – the addition of images and text appropriately and creatively
SYSTEMS AND CONTROL – used to ensure quality and accuracy in the production of your prototype

---

8.3 PLANNING YOUR WORK, AND UNIT ASSESSMENT

LEARNING OUTCOMES

By the end of this section you should have developed a knowledge and understanding of:

- how to plan your work in this unit
- how the assessment criteria are applied to this unit
- how much portfolio work is required for this unit.

You will be allowed 20 hours in which to complete this unit. The work associated with this unit must be completed under your teacher's supervision. However, some of your research work, by its very nature, may take place outside school under limited supervision. You must clearly reference the source of any information you use within your portfolio.

A maximum of 60 marks will be awarded for this task, which will form 30% of the total marks for a full-course GCSE.

▶ Planning your approach

It is always useful to have a look at the way the unit is to be assessed before you start. In this way you can make sure you spend an appropriate amount of time on each section of the unit based on the amount of marks available. You also need to have an idea how much work you are expected to produce in the time available. As a guide, your portfolio should be no more than 15 sheets of A3, or equivalent A4 or electronic alternative.

Strands	Marks	Time	A3 or equivalent
Creativity	10	3	3
Designing	14	6	7
Making	28	9	3
Evaluating	8	2	2
TOTALS	60	20	15

Table 8.3 Marks–time work allocations for A531

EXAMINER'S TIPS

- Try to stick to the number of sheets of A3 suggested per section. Use all the space on every sheet.
- You should be concise, and edit your work as you go.
- Plan your time carefully, and stick to it – overruns will mean that later sections are rushed or missed out altogether.
- Always allow time for the evaluation section – too many students run out of time and leave this section out.
- Aim for quality in your work, not quantity.

KEY POINTS

- You have 20 hours in which to complete this controlled assessment unit.
- There is a maximum of 60 marks available.
- The unit represents 30% of your full-course GCSE.

▶ 8.4 ASSESSMENT EVIDENCE AND MARK ALLOCATION

LEARNING OUTCOMES

By the end of this section you should have developed a knowledge and understanding of:

- how this unit is assessed
- the evidence needed for each strand of assessment.

The unit is broken down into four strands:

1. Creativity
2. Designing
3. Making
4. Evaluation.

Each strand has the allocation of marks given below.

▌ Creativity (10 marks)

You should spend no more than 3 hours on this section. You should:

- select a theme and, from that, identify a product/starting point
- identify and apply the principles of good design
- identify potential users – their needs and wants
- identify trends in existing products
- produce a design brief.

▌ Designing (14 marks)

You should spend no more than 6 hours on this section. You should:

- produce a response to the design brief through analysis
- produce a detailed specification
- produce creative and original design ideas
- use a number of drawing/presentation techniques, including CAD
- explain your choice of design.

▌ Making (28 marks)

You should spend no more than 9 hours on this section. You should:

- plan the production of your prototype
- select appropriate materials
- select the tools, processes and techniques you will use
- carry out a risk assessment to ensure safe working
- show that you can solve technical problems
- record the stages in the making of your prototype.

▌ Evaluation (8 marks)

You should spend no more than 2 hours on this section. You should:

- critically evaluate the processes involved in making your prototype
- suggest modifications to improve the making process.

▌ How this unit is assessed

This unit will be marked by your teacher according to the **assessment criteria** for the unit, using a 'best fit 'approach. For each of the assessment criteria, one of the descriptors provided in the marking grid that most closely describes the quality of your work will be selected. The marking should be positive, rewarding your achievements rather than penalising any failures or omissions.

Basic ability	Demonstrates ability	Works competently with independence
CREATIVITY Show simple/limited understanding of the principles of good design and shows limited awareness of the user.	CREATIVITY Can identify the principles of good design and can relate products to users' needs.	CREATIVITY Identifies and applies the principles of good design and clearly relates products to users' needs and wants.
Identify one or two trends in existing solutions and use this understanding in a design context. [0–3]	Demonstrate the significance of trends in existing products; interpret and apply this understanding in a design context. [4–7]	Demonstrate and understand the significance of trends in existing solutions; reinterpret and apply this understanding in imaginative ways. [8–10]
DESIGNING Demonstrate a limited response to a brief and produce a simple specification for a prototype product.	DESIGNING Demonstrate an appropriate response to a brief and produce a suitable specification for a prototype product as a result of analysis.	DESIGNING Demonstrate an appropriate and considered response to a brief and produce a detailed specification for a prototype product as a result of analysis.
Produce one or two simple design ideas using a limited range of skills and techniques including the use of ICT.	Produce creative ideas and communicate these by using appropriate skills and techniques including the use of ICT.	Produce creative and original ideas by generating, developing and communicating designs using appropriate skills and techniques including the use of ICT.
Using drawing and annotation gives limited details of the chosen prototype production. [0–4]	Using drawing and annotation communicates adequate details of the design chosen for prototype production. [5–10]	Using drawing and annotation clearly communicates full details of the design chosen for prototype production. [11–14]
MAKING Limited modelling of the final prototype	MAKING Use modelling to identify problems and consider the suitability of the product for the user.	MAKING Use modelling to identify problems and make appropriate modifications, assess the suitability of the product considering, in detail, the needs of the user.

Basic ability	Demonstrates ability	Works competently with independence
Select appropriate materials.	Select appropriate materials.	Select appropriate materials.
Select tools and equipment as appropriate to the material area.	Select tools and equipment as appropriate to the material area.	Select tools and equipment as appropriate to the material area.
Work safely to produce a low- quality prototype.	Work effectively and safely to produce a reasonable quality prototype.	Work skilfully and safely to produce a high-quality prototype suitable for the intended user.
Surface graphics demonstrate a basic level of competence.	Surface graphics are adequate and demonstrate competency.	Surface graphics are appropriate and demonstrate a high level of competency.
Use workshop/design studio facilities as appropriate to graphics.[0–6]	Choose and use workshop/design studio facilities as appropriate to graphics. [7–13]	Assess and apply knowledge in the workshop/design studio facilities as appropriate to graphics. [14–20]
Demonstrate a simple understanding of how to solve a technical problem as it arises. [0–1]	Demonstrate a practical understanding and ability in solving some technical problems as they arise. [2–3]	Demonstrate a practical and thorough understanding and ability in solving technical problems effectively and efficiently as they arise. [4]
Simply record the creation of the product using notes and/or visual evidence. [0–1]	Record key stages involved in the creation of the prototype, provide notes and visual evidence. [2–3]	Record key stages involved in creation of the prototype, provide comprehensive notes and visual evidence. [4]
CRITICAL EVALUATION Give a limited evaluation of the modelling and prototyping process.	CRITICAL EVALUATION Give an evaluation of the making process. Reflect on how to improve the modelling and prototyping process.	CRITICAL EVALUATION Critically evaluate the processes involved in the designing and making the prototype. Reflect and suggest modifications to improve the modelling and prototyping process.

Basic ability	Demonstrates ability	Works competently with independence
There will be little or no use of specialist terms.	There will be some use of specialist terms, although specialist terms, although these may not always be appropriate.	Specialist terms will be used appropriately and correctly.
Answers may be ambiguous and disorganised.	The information will be presented, for the most part in a structured format.	The information will be presented in a structured format.
Errors of spelling, punctuation and grammar may be intrusive. [0–2]	There may be occasion errors in spelling, punctuation and grammar. [3–5]	The candidate can demonstrate the accurate use of spelling, punctuation and grammar. [6–8]

Table 8.4 Marking criteria for Unit A531

KEY POINTS

- Each strand of the unit has key sections that must be completed.
- You should limit the amount of time spent on each element, based on the marks awarded for each section.
- This unit is marked by your teacher using assessment criteria provided by OCR.
- The marks for your work will be awarded by comparing how the quality of your work 'best fits' with the assessment descriptors.

EXAMINER'S TIPS

- Apportion your time carefully, and stick to it.
- Be concise and selective in your presentation of your design – always explain/justify the inclusion of anything in your folio.
- Make sure you thoroughly plan and record the production of your product.
- Explain your design ideas and choice of outcome.
- Use a variety of drawing/presentation techniques, including ICT.
- Avoid elaborate borders and unnecessary colour/shading.
- Aim to produce a high-quality product.
- Always ensure that you leave enough time to produce a critical evaluation that includes suggested modifications.
- Use the assessment criteria to self-assess your work as you complete each strand of the assessment.

KEY TERM

ASSESSMENT CRITERIA – how the marks for each section are awarded

CHAPTER 9

UNIT A532: SUSTAINABLE DESIGN

9.1 AN OVERVIEW OF UNIT A532: SUSTAINABLE DESIGN

By the end of this section you should have developed a knowledge and understanding of:

- how this unit fits into your qualification
- how the unit is assessed.

*Unit A532: Sustainable design is one of four units that you will need to study to gain a GCSE **qualification** in Design and Technology: Graphics (J303). If you study the GCSE (short course) in Design and Technology: Graphics (J043) you will need to study this unit and unit A531.*

▶ Assessment of this unit

Assessment of this **unit** is through a 60-minute externally set and marked **exam**. The exam can be taken in January and June each year. You are allowed to take the exam twice, with the highest score counting towards your qualification. Your teacher will help you decide if you are ready to take the exam.

The exam will contain a number of questions that focus on sustainable design.

KEY POINTS

Unit A532: Sustainable Design is:

- assessed through a 60-minute exam available in January and June
- one of four units required for a GCSE in Design and Technology: Graphics (J303)
- one of two units required for a GCSE (short course) in Design and Technology: Graphics (J043).

KEY TERMS

QUALIFICATION – a GCSE or GCSE short course
TEST – work done under controlled conditions
UNIT – part of a qualification

EXAMINER'S TIPS

You should prepare for the exam by:

- looking back at the notes you made in the mini-tasks you have undertaken
- working through past exam papers and exemplar questions
- asking your teacher what you need to do to be ready to take the exam.

9.2 SUSTAINABLE DESIGN

LEARNING OUTCOME

By the end of this section you should have developed a knowledge and understanding of:

- what is meant by sustainable design.

*Sustainable design is a way of thinking that supports responsible designing and making that does not have a negative impact on the **environment**, **society** and the **economy***.

Sustainability

This unit aims to develop your knowledge and understanding of sustainability, environmental concerns, **cultural** issues, **moral issues** and **social issues**. In order to do this you should:

- consider how design and technology has **evolved**, through analysis of products from the past and present
- consider how future designs will impact on the world in which we live
- study examples of both old and new products to gain awareness and understanding of trends and innovations in **design** and manufacture

Figure 9.1 Products have evolved

- consider the impact that the design of products has on the environment, society and the economy.

To develop a **sustainable** approach to design you must think very carefully about the:

- choice and use of materials
- manufacturing methods
- use of the product
- **disposal** of the product.

Products that waste material, use large

amounts of energy or create excessive pollution cannot be sustained over a long period of time.

KEY POINTS

Sustainable design:

- is a way of thinking that supports responsible designing and making
- is concerned with reducing the impact products have on the environment, society and the economy
- aims to develop your knowledge and understanding of environmental concerns, cultural issues, moral issues and social issues.

EXAMINER'S TIPS

Analyse existing products to:

- see how they have evolved
- assess the impact they have upon the world
- identify ways in which we might reduce the impact they have upon the environment, society and the economy.

KEY TERMS

CULTURAL – the ways and beliefs of a society

DESIGN – to plan something

DISPOSAL – what we do with products once they are no longer of use

ECONOMY – concerned with money

ENVIRONMENT – the physical world in which we live

EVOLVE – to change over a period of time

MORAL ISSUE – deciding between right and wrong

SOCIAL ISSUE – concerned with the way people live

SOCIETY – the people who live in the environment

SUSTAINABLE – can be maintained over a period of time

SUSTAINABLE DESIGN – a way of thinking that supports responsible designing of products that do not have a negative impact on the environment, society and economy

QUESTIONS

1. Consider how mobile telephones have developed over the last few years. What are the trends? What have been the benefits to society? Have there been any negative effects?

2. Discuss ways in which designers could reduce the impact packaging has on the environment, society and the economy by using more recycled materials.

9.3 WHAT DO I NEED TO KNOW FOR THE EXAM?

LEARNING OUTCOME

By the end of this section you should have developed a knowledge and understanding of:

- the content of this unit.

*The **content** of this unit is divided into the following sections:*

- *the '6Rs' (Recycle, Reuse, Reduce, Refuse, Rethink, Repair)*
- *product analysis and the design of products.*

The 6Rs

RECYCLE	How easy is it to take apart? How can the parts be used again? How much energy to reprocess parts?
REUSE	Which parts can I use again? Has it another valuable use without processing it?
REDUCE	Which parts are not needed? Do we need as much material? Can we simplify the product?
REFUSE	Is it really necessary? Is it going to last? Is it fair trade? Is it unfashionable to be trendy and too costly to be stylish?
RETHINK	How can it do the job better? Is it energy efficient? Has it been designed for disassembly?
REPAIR	Which parts can be replaced? Which parts are going to fail? How easy is it to replace parts?

Figure 9.2 The 6Rs

Recycle

Recycle is what we do with the objects we use in our daily lives. Recycling is the conversion of waste products into new materials. This is done to extend the life and usefulness of a product that seems to have no further purpose. Recycling means reusing a product, but sometimes before a product can be reused it will need to undergo processing or treatment. The three main types of recycling are primary recycling, secondary or physical recycling and tertiary or chemical recycling.

Primary recycling

The second-hand use of items or products is a form of primary recycling as the items are simply being used again. Charity shops stock a large selection of recycled products. Giving items to friends and relatives, or selling them on internet auction sites, are all ways of primary recycling.

Secondary or physical recycling

This is the process by which waste materials are recycled into different types of products. For example, a large corriflute sign could be cut up and used for labels for plants. The change the product will go through depends

Figure 9.3 Clothing rail

on the main fibre or material of the product. Some products can be left to biodegrade before being regenerated into something else.

Tertiary or chemical recycling

This is when products are broken down and reformulated – for example, plastic bottles can be recycled into fibres and then re-spun into polyester to make fleece fabric used for coats and blankets. Car tyres can be reused to make numerous products (e.g. computer mouse mats).

Figure 9.4 Old tyres

Recyclable materials include: glass, paper, metals, wood, textiles, electronics, tyres, plastics and food waste. Indeed, most, if not all, things can be recycled in some way.

Figure 9.5 Paper being recycled at waste-collection plant

Why recycle?

Everything we dispose of goes somewhere, although once the container or bag of rubbish is out of our hands and out of our houses we forget it instantly. Our consumer lifestyle is rapidly filling up rubbish dumps all over the world and, as this happens, our concerns about the environment grow. When designing and making a new product, designers and manufacturers need to consider how their product can be recycled at the end of its life cycle.

Figure 9.6 Recycling: plastic, metal, glass and paper

You will need to have knowledge of the following:

- materials that can be recycled
- products that use recycled materials
- disassembly – reprocessing materials for use in new products.

Reuse

Products that can be **reused** for either the same purpose or a new purpose

Products that are designed to be **reused** result in less waste. This leads to conservation of materials and resources. Many places around the UK collect unwanted products, or repair them for redistribution for the same or a similar end use.

Products that can be adapted to suit an alternative use

Some local areas have set up their own websites and organisations for the reuse of unwanted items; these are used and run by groups of people who actively aim to adapt existing products for alternative uses.

Reduce

The life cycle of a product

A new product progresses through a variety of stages, from the original idea to its decline, where it might be discontinued or disposed of. You must consider the impact of a product on the environment and its impact on society as a whole. The main stages involved are as follows.

- The raw materials: how are they harvested/made?
- The production process: how is the product made?
- Transport and distribution: you need to consider what, how, where and the cost

- Uses: what are the intended uses of the product? How will it be used by the client or customer?
- Recycling: how can the product be recycled?
- Care and maintenance: what is needed, how much, and is it environmentally friendly?
- Disposal: the waste from manufacturing or the product itself. Ask yourself the question 'Is it recyclable or biodegradable?'

Eco footprint

This is the term used to refer to the measurement of the effect of our actions on the environment. You as a designer must consider the effect of your product on the environment from the first stages of your design ideas through to the final making and eventual disposal or recycling of your product. Your footprint involves showing that you have designed the product with the environment in mind, and have tried to minimise the damage caused by the various stages throughout your product's life cycle.

Built-in obsolescence

This is where the product has been designed to last for a set period of time. The functions of the product have been designed by the manufacturer to fail after a certain time limit. The consumer is then under pressure to purchase again. This built-in obsolescence is in many different products, from vehicles to light bulbs and items of clothing, and in food 'use by' or 'best before' dates. Manufacturers can invest money to make the product obsolete faster, by making it with cheaper components that might be less reliable.

Energy and waste in production process

The consumption of non-renewable energy resources such as coal and oil is causing an energy crisis. These resources will eventually run out. Using non-renewable resources adds to pollution problems as products made from oil often take a long time to break down in the environment.

The transportation of products is a high user of oil and petrol – refined fossil fuels. 'Green energy' is the leader of alternative energy sources, which are considered environmentally friendly and non-polluting. Energy can be generated from natural sources such as:

- wind power
- solar power
- geothermal
- hydro power
- tidal/wave.

Figure 9.7 Wind turbines

Materials: waste

We often overlook how much we waste as consumers, whether it be consumable products, or power sources such as electricity or packaging. Waste management is a growing problem, from chemicals that get into the water system, to paper and card used in packaging. Switching off our computers or not leaving the television on standby can help us to **reduce** the amount of energy wasted. Reusing carrier bags or buying locally made products all helps reduce material waste and bring about a more eco-friendly footprint. Manufacturers now have to follow guidelines on how to get rid of their waste effluent. Research into the effective management of pollution, energy and other material waste is constantly ongoing. You need to be aware of current changes within these areas.

Refuse

Issues relating to sustainable design

The processing, manufacturing, packaging and transport of our products uses huge amounts of energy and can create lots of waste. You need to look at the sustainability of a product from an environmental and social viewpoint. How is the product made and can we ensure that little or no harm is created in the environment by this method of manufacture? Sometimes a choice between the performance of the product required and the impact on the environment as a result of its manufacture has to be considered and debated.

Materials we should refuse to use

Why should you **refuse** to use some products? The answer includes a variety of reasons.

- It may be because the product is made unnecessarily from a manmade source instead of natural.
- It might be because of the toxic chemicals used in the product.
- What about the manufacturing process itself – has it been made under appropriate safety regulations?
- What about the rights of the workers and the conditions they have been working in?

- Packaging and transport distances and costs.
- It might not be good for you (e.g. high fat content).

You should think about these issues before you accept a product and, above all, do not buy it if you do not need it!

Rethink

Within your own lifestyle and that of others close to you, you need to **rethink** about your lifestyle and the way in which you buy products and the energy required to use them. Society is constantly evolving and changing, and you can evaluate how you could make a difference.

- How is it possible to approach design problems differently? What ideas can you develop to ensure a difference?
- Using an existing product that has become waste; using the materials or components for another purpose without processing them. What can you design? What could be designed?

Repair

Today's throwaway society means it is quicker and easier to throw something away rather than **repair** it. We looked at built-in obsolescence earlier in this chapter, where manufacturers encourage consumers to repurchase rather than repair.

- Some products you can repair yourself, some we can take to repair shops.
- Some products are beyond repair or would cost too much to fix.
- Unwanted electronic and electrical equipment is the fastest-growing waste area. Why? The need to change attitudes to this is pressing. How might you do this?

▶ Product analysis and the design of products

Social issues

Figure 9.8 Logo depicting global unity

Today we live in a global society. You need to be aware of the ways this can affect the designing of products. Products need to be designed for use by a range of different **cultures** and nationalities, all of which may have different specific needs. Society today has become multicultural and diverse; some products may be designed for a specific section of society, others may be universal across all.

When designing, bear in mind:

- social development – through recognising the need to consider the views of others when designing and discussing designed products
- the relationship between man and the general environment
- the economic development cycle of a range of products, and the impact on individuals, societies and countries
- issues associated with economic development and employment (e.g. where a product is made, costs of components,

materials, manufacturing including labour and transportation of the finished product)

- the values of society – why we wear clothes (e.g. for protection, modesty, adornment); clothing, for example, has become a way of reflecting our gender, culture and religion; some items have become unisex and are used across all of society.

Moral issues

Moral issues are concerned with the way in which products are manufactured, and the way in which they affect the safety, comfort and well-being of the people who make them and those who come into contact with the designs/products. Many companies now follow a code of practice to try to ensure that products are made in the right conditions without exploiting workers. Companies will consider:

- moral development, reflecting on how technology affects the environment, and the advantages and disadvantages of new technologies for local and national communities

- conditions of working within a manufacturing environment (e.g. job satisfaction, wages, safety of the workplace and workers)

- the Ethical Trading Initiative (ETI), which is an alliance of companies, non-governmental organisations (NGOs) and trade union organisations; its aim is to promote and improve the implementation of regulated codes of practice that set out minimal working requirements; its useful website is at www.ethicaltrade.org.

Ethical companies ensure that their employees have basic labour rights, and also take care to protect the environment in the production, packaging and distribution of their goods. Such companies are often termed **'sweatshop** free'.

The Fairtrade Foundation is the independent non-profit organisation that licenses use of the FAIRTRADE Mark on products in the UK, in accordance with internationally agreed Fairtrade standards. The Foundation was established in 1992. Its website is at www.fairtrade.org.uk.

Figure 9.9 FAIRTRADE Mark

Cultural issues

Many cultures have important traditions that form part of their identity. How do products affect the quality of lives within different cultures? The use and maintenance of traditional skills and cultural knowledge can have an impact on modern products.

- Look at, respond to and value the responses of others to design solutions.

- Think about the impact of different cultures on modern products – the use and maintenance of traditional skills and knowledge.

Culture is about the way that people behave and relate to one another. It is about the way that people live, work and spend their leisure time. It is about people's beliefs and aspirations.

Environmental issues

In a modern, fast-changing society, where products are continually being changed, it is important that you keep up to date with various issues. You will need to address the following key areas:

- Understand and be able to select materials that are both suitable and sustainable.

- Be aware of the disposal and recycling of materials and components, and the appropriate methods of manufacture.

- Prepare materials economically, minimising waste and using pre-manufactured standard components.

- Have knowledge of the reduction of common use of environmentally unfriendly chemicals and materials dangerous to the environment (e.g. bleaches, CFCs, toxic materials). High levels of pollution can be caused by manufacturing, and ways to reduce this are being investigated. It is sometimes necessary to use chemicals and manmade materials that are not the most ecologically sound, if the specific performance characteristic of that chemical/material can be obtained only in that way.

CFCs

CFCs are one of a group of synthetic substances containing chlorine and bromine, developed in the 1930s. Thought to be safe, non-flammable and non-toxic, they were widely used until the 1980s, when it was discovered that they were the main source of harm to the ozone layer.

Carbon footprint

This is a measure of the impact human activities have on the environment, in terms of the amount of greenhouse gases produced through the release of carbon dioxide. This is all having an impact on global warming. A carbon footprint is linked to the ecological footprint, and can be measured in terms of the transportation of materials and goods, energy use in manufacture, and the use of natural resources and renewable resources.

Figure 9.10 Carbon footprint logo

Carbon offsetting

This is a method by which people and companies can undertake measures to offset the impact they have on the environment in terms of their carbon footprint. Carbon offsetting involves contributing to the development of more ecological methods of energy generation, such as the use of renewable sources.

Reforestation

Reforestation is the term used to describe the restocking of existing forests and woodlands. The advantage of this method is that the areas restocked can provide the ecosystem with resource benefits to soak up

Figure 9.11 Symbols used in packaging

some of the negative effects of carbon dioxide.

End of life disposal

This issue is linked to the need to dispose of redundant products and their packaging in a safe and environmentally friendly way. The use of labelling for symbols for specific packaging is helpful to the consumer when buying products.

Design issues

Buying a product can be expensive, so you need to ensure that you have got what you want and that it will benefit you in some way. Researching the product beforehand, and analysing the information gathered, can help you draw a conclusion that ensures your choice is successful.

Designers are constantly changing and evolving their work. Sources of inspiration come from all design and technology areas. In all products, new and constantly changing materials are being developed. Smart materials and modern materials have developed massively over the last few years.

Eco-design

This involves the whole system of looking at an end product, from design to finished article, its use of materials and energy. Eco-design is the process of designing a product from scratch with the environment in mind, and trying to minimise the damage caused to the environment by the product's **life cycle**. A designer must think through the following main stages if the product is to be successful and acceptable as eco-designed:

* product planning
* product development
* design process
* functionality
* safety
* ergonomics
* technical issues and requirements
* design aesthetics.

The European Ecolabel is an official label awarded to a product guaranteeing it has fulfilled specific criteria. A product awarded the Ecolabel will have been found to have a smaller environmental impact than other similar products. The Ecolabel is the official sign of environmental quality. It is awarded by independent organisations and is valid throughout Europe. The label's criteria aim to limit the environmenal impacts of a product over its entire life cycle by looking at such issues as water consumption, waste production and the use of renewable resources.

Figure 9.12 European eco-label

Globalisation is the internationalisation of products, labour and skills throughout the world. Products are made in countries where specific traditions, skills and techniques, which are part of people's everyday lives, can give valuable income and jobs to a previously poor area. Manufacturers can take advantage of low labour costs. Different cultures have different needs, and what is a requirement of one culture can be very different from that of another.

▶ Summary

Many areas in this chapter are also covered in more detail in other chapters. Where possible, these have been cross-referenced for you. Sustainable design is a world issue and a constantly changing one. You should want the world to be a great, sustainable place to live in, one that is for you, your friends and relatives, and for future generations.

A sustainable way of designing can have an impact and positive effect on everyone. As a designer, you need to remember and consider the social, economic and environmental implications of your decisions.

KEY TERMS

CARBON FOOTPRINT – measurement of the impact of human activities on the environment

CARBON OFFSETTING – actions to offset the impact people have on the environment

CFCs – one of a group of synthetic substances containing chlorine and bromine, developed in the 1930s; thought to be safe, non-flammable and non-toxic, they were widely used until the 1980s, when it was discovered that they were the main source of harm to the ozone layer

CONTENT – body of information you need to know in order to sit the test

CULTURE – the way that people behave and relate to one another; it is about the way that people live, work and spend their leisure time, and people's beliefs and aspirations

ECO-DESIGN – designing a product with the environment in mind

GLOBALISATION – the internationalisation of products

LIFE CYCLE – the stages a new product goes through, from conception to eventual decomposition

RECYCLE – to reprocess materials to make another product

REDUCE – to lessen the amount used

REFORESTATION – the restocking of existing forests and woodlands

REFUSE – to not accept, or to say no

REPAIR – to mend something

RETHINK – to look at a new way of doing something

REUSE – to use again

SWEATSHOP – a business with poor working conditions

KEY POINT

All the content can be examined in the end-of-unit exam so make sure you have knowledge and understanding of all the key areas covered above.

EXAMINER'S TIPS

To be successful in the end-of-unit exam you should have:

- considered all areas of the unit content
- applied the content to a number of different situations through mini-tasks.

QUESTIONS

1. What does the term recycling mean?

2. List three materials that can be recycled.

3. Name a material made from recycled products.

4. How do methods of transportation harm the environment?

5. What alternative sources of energy are available? Identify how good design and product choice improve the quality of life.

6. Look at the way that designers respond to changing styles, taste, technological advances and environmental pressures. What impact does this have?

9.4 HOW TO PREPARE FOR THE EXAM

LEARNING OUTCOME

By the end of this section you should have developed a knowledge and understanding of:

- how to prepare for this unit exam.

*The best way to **prepare** for this unit exam is through a number of mini-tasks.*

▶ Mini-tasks

Mini-tasks are short tasks that are around 2–6 hours in length. They should include opportunities for:

- group discussion
- working with ideas and media
- researching concepts
- recording information
- visits to technology innovation centres, industry, local councils, museums, etc.

Over a period of time, the mini-tasks will cover the course content. You should collect evidence from the mini-tasks in the form of **research** reports, which can then be used for the end-of-unit exam preparation.

Figure 9.13 Mini-tasks

1	Sustainable design	✓
2	The 6 R's	
3	Transport project	
4	Moral and social issues	
5	Design issues	✓
6	Design for living	
7	Recycling materials	✓
8	Material selection	

Figure 9.14 Covering the content

KEY POINTS

- Preparation for the unit exam should be through a series of mini-tasks.
- Over a period of time, the mini-tasks will cover the course content.
- Your notes from the mini-tasks are important because you can use them for exam preparation.

EXAMINER'S TIPS

- Keep a record of the mini-tasks you have undertaken.
- Record what you have done or found out in each of the mini-tasks.
- Make a tick list to check you have covered the unit content.

KEY TERMS

PREPARE – to get ready
RESEARCH – collecting and analysing information

QUESTION

1. Explore the concept of making furniture from recycled card. You should produce a report under the following headings:
- Types of material available
- Environmental, social and economic benefits of using these materials

- Structural stability, joining methods and finish
- Ideas for seating.

9.5 THE EXAM

LEARNING OUTCOMES

By the end of this section you should have developed a knowledge and understanding of:

- the exam structure
- the types of question that will be asked.

This unit exam is worth 20% of the total marks for the full GCSE course, and 40% for the short course.

▶ The exam structure

This unit is assessed by a 60-minute exam that is divided into section A and section B. You should spend about 20 minutes on section A and 40 minutes on section B. The marks available for each question are shown in square brackets [ ].

The quality of written communication is assessed in this unit.

Section A
Section A consists of 15 short-answer questions worth a total of 15 marks.

An example of a section A question

A biodegradable material will:

(a) naturally grow in cold climates

(b) naturally rot in the environment

(c) be reusable as a different product

(d) not grow in hot climates

The correct answer is (b) and this would score 1 mark.

Section B

Section B contains three questions worth 15 marks each. Answers require you to **sketch**, **annotate** and **write** short sentences or longer written answers. An example of a section B question is:

Eco design is about designing a product with the environment in mind and trying to minimise the damage to the environment throughout a product's life cycle.

(a) Explain what the following areas are in the design process.

Product planning:

....

.... [2]

Development:

....

.... [2]

Functionality:

....

.... [2]

Safety:

....

.... [2]

Aesthetics:

....

.... [2]

A manufacturer wishes to develop a range of environmentally friendly products to be sold in a shop at a museum.

(b) Name your product.

.... [1]

(c) Identify **four** specification points for your chosen design product.

1 .... [1]

2 .... [1]

3 .... [1]

4 .... [1]

Total [15]

There is more than one correct answer to this type of question. You will need to think about the mini-tasks you have already undertaken and apply the knowledge to this design situation.

KEY POINTS

Remember, the unit exam is:

- available in January and June
- 60 minutes long
- divided into section A and section B
- section A is worth 15 marks and section B 45 marks
- section A contains 15 short questions
- section B contains three longer questions.

EXAMINER'S TIPS

- Work through specimen questions before the exam.
- Read the questions very carefully before you start the exam.
- Identify the key words, such as 'sketch' or 'annotate', in each question.

KEY TERMS

ANNOTATE – add notes to a drawing or sketch

SKETCH – make a freehand drawing

CHAPTER 10

UNIT A533: MAKING QUALITY PRODUCTS

10.1 AN OVERVIEW OF UNIT A533: MAKING QUALITY PRODUCTS

By the end of this section you should have developed a knowledge and understanding of:

- how this unit fits into your qualification
- how the unit is assessed.

Unit A533: Making Quality Products is one of four units that you will need to study to gain a GCSE qualification in Design and Technology: Graphics.

▶ Overview

Assessment of this **unit** is through a 20-hour controlled assessment. The assessment can be taken in January and June. You are allowed to take the assessment twice, with the highest score counting towards your **qualification**. Your teacher will help you decide if you are ready to undertake the work for this unit.

You are required to research, **design** and make a functioning prototype product.

You must select one of the **themes** that are published by OCR as a starting point for the task. The themes are reviewed periodically. Your teacher will be able to give you the current list of OCR published themes.

Your school is allowed to contextualise the theme and the starting point appropriately to reflect its own or community resources, and access to local business and industry that may add realism to your work. The task can be linked to your interests or other influences such as competitions, commerce or the community. You are not allowed to use the same theme for this unit as submitted or intended for submission for Unit A531.

Exemplar products	Graphic themes
Promotional mobile	A promotional '3D mobile' as a novelty item to promote and/or raise awareness of a specific organisation or issue.
Packaging	An item of attractive and protective packaging for a specific three-dimensional product.
'Press-out' model	A range of children's books is being launched. Each book contains a specific press-out item that can be assembled without the use adhesives or scissors.
Theatre or concert staging	A stage or studio set design for a specific production.
Exhibition stands	An innovative and eye-catching exhibition stand for a specific organisation to display a new product.
'Pop-up' book	An educational book for children incorporating a range of different and interesting 'pop-up' mechanisms.
Modern architectural building	Docklands in London is home to some of the UK's most interesting and innovative buildings. Design a modern office block, school, shopping centre or other large building for a modern city.
Point of sale display	An eye-catching and effective method of displaying and promoting a new product to people.
Flat-pack carrying aids	A flat-pack carrying aid that allows a number of potentially difficult items to be carried easily in one hand.
Recycling/sustainability	Choose an existing graphic product that is difficult to recycle. Re-design it to make it recyclable/reuseable.

Table 10.1 Unit A533 controlled assessment themes for 2010

Aims of this assessment

This unit aims to assess your ability to:

- develop and demonstrate designing skills
- demonstrate good making and workshop skills
- demonstrate critical evaluation skills.

You will be required to produce:

- a production plan
- a number of concise worksheets or design presentation boards (A3, A4 or digital equivalent), showing design development and **modelling**, which may include the use of ICT to support the design process

- a product capable of evaluation
- a minimum of two digital photographs of your product, showing the front and back views of the product in use
- digital images/photographs of any models/mock-ups used when designing, modelling or testing
- a completed OCR cover sheet.

Submission of controlled assessment work

Your **controlled assessment** work can be submitted on paper or in electronic format but not a mixture of the two.

Work submitted on paper

A 'Contents' page with a numbering system should be included to aid organisation. All your work should be on the same-size paper but it does not matter what size paper you use. You can produce your work by hand or using ICT.

Work submitted electronically

Your work will need to be organised in folders so that the evidence can be accessed easily by a teacher or moderator. This structure is commonly known as a folder tree. There should be a top-level folder detailing your centre number, candidate number, surname and forename, together with the unit code A533. The next folder down should be called 'Home Page', which will be an index of all your work. The evidence for each section of the work should then be contained in a separate folder, containing appropriately named files. These files can be from the Microsoft Office suite, Movie, Audio, Graphics, Animation, Structured Mark-up or Text formats. PowerPoint is an ideal platform for producing electronic portfolios.

KEY POINTS

Unit A533: Making Quality Products:

- one of four units required for a GCSE in Design and Technology: Graphics
- assessed through a 20-hour controlled assessment available in January and June
- marked by your teachers and **externally moderated** by OCR examiners.

EXAMINER'S TIPS

You should:

- Prepare for the assessment by looking back over past design and make tasks.
- Check with your teacher well in advance of the assessment dates to see what you need to do in order to be ready to take the assessment.
- Plan how you will use the time available for the assessment task.
- Always explain your ideas thoroughly and concisely. Do not assume the reader has any knowledge of what you are doing.

KEY TERMS

CONTROLLED ASSESSMENT – work done under controlled conditions, authenticated as the student's own work

DESIGN – to plan something

EXTERNALLY MODERATED – sent to OCR for standardisation of marks

MODELLING – models that help test an idea

QUALIFICATION – a GCSE or GCSE short course

THEME – starting point of the task

UNIT – part of a qualification

10.2 WHAT DO I NEED TO DO FOR THIS UNIT?

By the end of this section you should have developed a knowledge and understanding of:

- the task you are required to undertake
- how to choose a theme
- what is an 'acceptable' graphic outcome.

The task that you undertake for this unit requires you to:

- *design for a need*
- *work with tools and equipment*
- *make a quality product*
- *evaluate the product.*

Selecting a theme

To be successful in this unit you should choose a theme that:

- you can identify a product or starting point for
- best suits your capabilities and interests
- best suits the resources of your school/college
- brings out the best of your ability.

Graphic product outcomes

Graphic outcomes may be either two- or three-dimensional products that must be made from compliant materials. Compliant materials must be able to be shaped, folded, cut and joined. The compliant materials for this unit are paper, card/board, foam board, thin sheet plastic, rigid foam, smart materials and appropriate pre-manufactured components.

Graphic materials	Paper Card and board Foam board Sheet plastic – up to 2 mm thick Rigid foam
Joining materials	PVA adhesive, spray adhesive, solvent cement, hot melt glue (glue gun), epoxy resin, glue sticks, single and double sided tape, Velcro, double sided sticky pads, paper fasteners, eyelets, press fit 'click' fasteners, Clic rivets (plastic rivets)
Smart and modern materials	Polymorph, thermochromic inks, pigments and film, photochromic inks and pigments, phosphorent pigments, fluorescent pigments, other 'Smart' and modern materials as they become available
Pre-manufactured components	Staples, press fasteners, plastic rivets, plastic nuts and bolts

Table 10.2 Compliant materials for Unit A533

▶ Assessment strands

You will be required to provide evidence for three separate assessment strands in this unit.

Strand 1: Develop and Demonstrate Designing Skills

- Use appropriate recording and drawing techniques.

- Produce a creative and considered response to a design brief.

- Produce a detailed specification for the product.

- Use detailed notes and annotated drawings to record original design ideas.

- Use **ICT/CAD/CAM** to support design development.

- Use drawing and annotation to clearly communicate details of the design chosen for production.

Strand 2: Demonstrate Good Making/Workshop Skills

- Use appropriate modelling or trialling techniques to aid product development.

- Plan, organise and record key manufacturing activities by means of comprehensive notes and photographic evidence.

- Make reasoned decisions about materials/components.

- Select appropriate tools and equipment.

- Work skilfully and safely to shape, form and finish materials, and assemble components.

- Apply knowledge of systems and control, ICT and new technologies as appropriate.

- Demonstrate a practical and thorough understanding and ability in solving technical problems effectively and efficiently as they arise.

- Complete product to a high quality standard

- Demonstrate ability to produce surface graphics to a high level of competency.

- Select appropriate materials.

Strand 3: Demonstrate Critical Evaluation Skills

- Evaluate the product against the specification.

- Undertake detailed testing and present meaningful conclusions.

KEY POINTS

- There are three strands to this unit: Develop and Demonstrate Designing Skills, Demonstrate Good Making/Workshop Skills and Demonstrate Critical **Evaluation** Skills. Your work should address each of these strands.

- Your graphic outcome may be either two- or three-dimensional.

- Your graphic outcome must be made from the compliant materials outlined in the **course specification**.

EXAMINER'S TIPS

- Keep an open mind at the start of the task.
- Organise your activity; use time effectively.
- The three strands form the basis of the task – do not leave any of them out.

KEY TERMS

CAD – computer-aided design

CAM – computer-aided manufacture

COURSE SPECIFICATION – the OCR booklet that outlines GCSE Design and Technology: Graphics

EVALUATION – asking how well the making process went

GRAPHIC OUTCOME – what you will make

ICT – information and communication technology

SURFACE GRAPHICS – the addition of images and text appropriately and creatively

SYSTEMS AND CONTROL – used to ensure quality and accuracy in the production of your prototype

QUESTIONS

1. In what three key strands does this unit assess you?

2. What are you required to produce for this unit?

10.3 PLANNING YOUR WORK, AND UNIT ASSESSMENT

LEARNING OUTCOMES

By the end of this section you should have developed a knowledge and understanding of:

- how to plan your work in this unit
- how the assessment criteria are applied to this unit
- how much portfolio work is required for this unit.

*You will be allowed 20 hours in which to complete this unit. The work associated with this unit must be completed under your teacher's supervision. However, some of your research work and **testing** of the product, by its very nature, may take place outside school under limited supervision. You must clearly reference the source of any information you use within your portfolio.*

A maximum of 60 marks will be awarded for this task, which will form 30% of the total marks for a full-course GCSE.

Planning your approach

It is always useful to have a look at the way the unit is to be assessed before you start. In this way you can make sure you spend an appropriate amount of time on each section of the unit based on the amount of marks available. You also need to have an idea how much work you are expected to produce in the time available. As a guide, your portfolio should be no more than 15 sheets of A3, or equivalent A4 or electronic alternative.

Strands	Marks	Time	A3 or equivalent
Designing	16	7	10
Making	36	11	3
Evaluating	8	2	2
TOTALS	60	20	15

Table 10.3 Marks–time work allocations for A533

KEY POINTS

- You have 20 hours in which to complete this controlled assessment unit.
- There is a maximum of 60 marks available.
- The unit represents 30% of your full-course GCSE.

KEY TERM

TESTING – finding out from users what they think of your product

EXAMINER'S TIPS

- Try to stick to the number of sheets of A3 suggested per section. Use all the space on every sheet.
- You should be concise, and edit your work as you go.
- Plan your time carefully, and stick to it – overruns will mean that later sections are rushed or missed out altogether.
- Always allow time for the evaluation section – too many students run out of time and leave this section out.
- Aim for quality in your work, not quantity.

10.4 ASSESSMENT EVIDENCE AND MARK ALLOCATION

LEARNING OUTCOMES

By the end of this section you should have developed a knowledge and understanding of:

- how this unit is assessed
- the evidence needed for each strand of assessment.

The unit is broken down into three strands:

1. Designing
2. Making
3. Evaluation.

Each strand has the allocation of marks given below.

Designing (16 marks)

You should spend no more than 7 hours on this section. You should:

- produce a design brief from your chosen theme
- produce a response to the design brief through analysis
- produce a detailed **specification**
- produce creative and original design ideas
- use a number of drawing/presentation techniques, including CAD
- explain your choice of design.

Making (36 marks)

You should spend no more than 11 hours on this section. You should:

- plan the production of your product
- select appropriate materials
- select the tools, processes and techniques you will use
- carry out a risk assessment to ensure safe working
- show that you can solve technical problems
- produce a high-quality product
- record the stages in the making of your product.

Evaluation (8 marks)

You should spend no more than 2 hours on this section. You should:

- critically evaluate the finished product against the specification
- undertake detailed testing and present meaningful conclusions leading to proposals for modifications to improve the product.

How this unit is assessed

This unit will be marked by your teacher according to the **assessment criteria** for the unit, using a 'best fit 'approach. For each of the assessment criteria, one of the descriptors provided in the marking grid that most closely describes the quality of your work will be selected. The marking should be positive, rewarding your achievements rather than penalising any failures or omissions.

KEY TERMS

ASSESSMENT CRITERIA – how the marks for each section are awarded

SPECIFICATION – the requirements of your chosen product

KEY POINTS

- Each strand of the unit has key sections that must be completed.
- You should limit the amount of time spent on each element, based on the marks awarded for each section.
- This unit is marked by your teacher using assessment criteria provided by OCR.
- The marks for your work will be awarded by comparing how the quality of your work 'best fits' with the assessment descriptors.

EXAMINER'S TIPS

- Apportion your time carefully, and stick to it.
- Be concise and selective in your presentation of your design – always explain/justify the inclusion of anything in your folio.
- Make sure you thoroughly plan and record the production of your product.
- Explain your design ideas and choice of outcome.
- Use a variety of drawing/presentation techniques, including ICT.
- Avoid elaborate borders and unnecessary colour/shading.
- Aim to produce a high-quality product.
- Always ensure that you leave enough time to produce a critical evaluation that includes suggested modifications.
- Use the assessment criteria to self-assess your work as you complete each strand of the assessment.

Basic ability	Demonstrates ability	Works competently with independence
DESIGNING Demonstrate a limited response to a brief and produce a simple specification for a product. **[0–1]**	**DESIGNING** Demonstrate an appropriate response to a brief and produce a suitable specification for a product as a result of analysis. **[2–3]**	**DESIGNING** Demonstrate an appropriate and considered response to a brief and produce a detailed specification for a product as a result of analysis. **[4]**
Produce one or two simple design ideas using a limited range of skills and techniques including using ICT.	Produce creative ideas and communicate these by using appropriate skills and techniques including the use of ICT.	Produce creative and original ideas by generating, developing and communicating designs using a range of appropriate skills and techniques including ICT.

Basic ability	Demonstrates ability	Works competently with independence
Using drawing and annotation communicates limited details of the chosen design proposal. [0–5]	Using drawing and annotation communicates adequate details of the chosen design proposal. [6–8]	Using drawing and annotation clearly communicates full details of the chosen design proposals. [9–12]
MAKING Plan and organise activities. Limited modelling of the final product.	MAKING Plan and organise activities. Use modelling to assess suitability of the product considering the needs of the user.	MAKING Plan and organise activities. Use modelling to assess the suitability of the product against the users needs, identify problems and make appropriate modifications.
Select appropriate materials.	Select appropriate materials.	Select appropriate materials.
Select hand and machine tools as appropriate to the material area.	Select hand and machine tools as appropriate to the material area.	Select hand and machine tools as appropriate to the material area.
Work safely to shape, form, assemble and finish materials or components as appropriate.	Work effectively and safely to shape, form, assemble and finish materials or components as appropriate.	Work skilfully and safely to shape, form, assemble and finish materials or components as appropriate.
Use workshop/design studio facilities as appropriate to material area.	Select and use workshop/ design studio facilities as appropriate to graphics.	Assess and apply knowledge in the workshop/design studio facilities as appropriate to graphics.
The product will exhibit a low standard of outcome and may not be successfully completed.	The product will be completed to a good standard and will meet most of the requirements of the final product specification.	The product will be completed to a high standard and will fully meet the requirements of the final product specification.
Surface graphics demonstrate a basic level of competency. [0–9]	Surface graphics are adequate and demonstrate competency. [10–17]	Surface graphics are appropriate and demonstrate a high level of competency. [18–24]
Demonstrate a simple understanding of how to solve a technical problem as they arise. [0–2]	Demonstrate a practical understanding and ability in solving some technical problems as they arise. [3–4]	Demonstrate a practical and thorough understanding and ability in solving technical problems effectively and efficiently as they arise. [5–6]

Basic ability	Demonstrates ability	Works competently with independence
Simply record the making of the product using notes and/or photographic evidence. **[0–2]**	Record key stages involved in the making of the product, provide notes and photographic evidence. **[3–4]**	Record key stages involved in making of the product, provide comprehensive notes and photographic evidence. **[5–6]**
CRITICAL EVALUATION Give a limited evaluation of the finished product with some reference to the specification. There is no evidence of testing the product in use. There will be little or no use of specialist terms. Answers may be ambiguous or disorganised. Errors of spelling, punctuation and grammar may be intrusive. **[0–2]**	CRITICAL EVALUATION Give an evaluation of the finished product with reference to the specification. Show superficial testing and reflect on how to improve the product. There will be some use of specialist terms, although these may not always be used appropriately. The information will be presented for the most part in a structured format. There will be occasional errors in spelling, punctuation and grammar. **[3–5]**	CRITICAL EVALUATION Critically evaluate the finished product against the specification. Undertake detailed testing; presenting meaningful conclusions leading to proposals for modifications to improve the product. Specialist terms will be used appropriately and correctly. The information will be presented in a structured format. The candidate can demonstrate the accurate use of spelling, punctuation and grammar. **[6–8]**

Table 10.4 Marking criteria for Unit A533

Figure 10.1 Michael's perfume box prototype

Figure 10.4 Abi's 'Day & Night' chocolate packaging (1)

Figure 10.2 Michael's perfume box prototype

Figure 10.5 Abi's 'Day & Night' chocolate packaging (2)

Figure 10.3 Chris's hair wax package

Figure 10.6 Paul's charity collection box

Figure 10.7 Alexander's soap packaging

Figure 10.10 Callum's aftershave packaging and point-of-sale display

Figure 10.8 Oliver's iPod packaging

Figure 10.11 Jordan's aftershave packaging and point-of-sale display

Figure 10.9 Part of Natalie's pop-up book

Figure 10.12 Leonie's perfume packaging and point-of-sale display

Figure 10.13 Alaa's perfume packaging and point-of-sale display

Figure 10.16 Noura's perfume packaging and point-of-sale display

Figure 10.14 Joshua's aftershave packaging and point-of-sale display

Figure 10.17 Sammi's CD case and point-of-sale display

Figure 10.15 Jessica's perfume packaging and point-of-sale display

Figure 10.18 Kieran's Styrofoam™ mould and vacuum-formed blister pack

CHAPTER 11

A534: TECHNICAL ASPECTS OF DESIGNING AND MAKING

11.1 OVERVIEW OF UNIT A534: TECHNICAL ASPECTS OF DESIGNING AND MAKING

By the end of this section you should have developed a knowledge and understanding of:

- how this unit fits into your qualification
- how the unit is assessed.

*Unit A534: Technical Aspects of Designing and Making is one of four units that you will need to study to gain a GCSE **qualification** in Design and Technology: Graphics (J303).*

KEY POINTS

This unit is:

- one of four units required for a GCSE in Design and Technology: Graphics
- assessed through a 75-minute exam.

▶ Assessment of this unit

Assessment of this **unit** is through a 75-minute externally set and marked exam. The **exam** can be taken in January or June. You are allowed to take the exam twice, with the highest score counting towards your qualification. Your teacher will help you decide if you are ready to take the exam.

The exam will contain a number of questions that focus on the technical aspects of designing and making.

EXAMINER'S TIPS

- Look back at the drawing, designing and making you have undertaken.
- Work through past exam papers and exemplar questions.
- Ask your teacher what you need to do to be ready to take the exam.

KEY TERMS

QUALIFICATION – a GCSE or GCSE short course
TEST – work done under controlled conditions
UNIT – part of a qualification

11.2 TECHNICAL ASPECTS OF DESIGNING AND MAKING

LEARNING OUTCOME

By the end of this section you should have developed a knowledge and understanding of:

- what is meant by the technical aspects of designing and making.

The technical aspects of designing and making are the knowledge, skills and understanding that underpin the design and manufacture of products made from graphic materials.

Technical aspects

In order to develop your **knowledge** and **understanding** of the **technical aspects** of designing and making you will need to:

- design and make quality manufactured products

- plan for the production of products, bearing in mind the use of time and resources

- consider the performance characteristics of different materials, including 'smart' and modern materials

- use tools and equipment, including new technologies and computer applications, to make quality manufactured products

- use and understand processes and techniques used to make quality manufactured products, both decorative and functional

- consider the impact that the use of graphic products has on the environment, including the need for sustainability

- consider health and safety issues.

You can develop this knowledge and understanding through:

- designing and making

- focused tasks

- specific theory lessons.

Your teacher will decide how to combine these activities to produce an exciting and interesting course.

KEY POINT

The key technical aspects are:

- materials, tools, equipment, processes and techniques that are required to make quality products.

EXAMINER'S TIP

The knowledge, **skills** and understanding that underpin the design and manufacture of products made from graphic materials need to be built up over a period of time. The more experiences you have in designing and making, the wider your knowledge will become.

Figure 11.1 Designing and making

KEY TERMS

KNOWLEDGE – the facts
SKILLS – things you can do
TECHNICAL ASPECT – scientific, practical or industrial knowledge
UNDERSTANDING – applying the facts to a new situation

11.3 WHAT DO I NEED TO KNOW FOR THE EXAM?

LEARNING OUTCOME

By the end of this section you should have developed a knowledge and understanding of:

- the content of this unit.

The content of this unit is divided into the following sections:

- *materials*
- *design*
- *product planning*
- *tools and equipment*
- *processes*
- *computer applications*
- *health and safety*
- *quality*
- *product analysis.*

▶ The content of the unit

The **content** of each section of this unit is shown below. Your teacher will set a number of designing and making tasks to help develop your knowledge and understanding of the materials and processes involved. You should keep copies of your work from these activities and use them for exam preparation.

You will need to develop your knowledge and understanding of the following areas.

Materials:

- the general classification of graphic materials
- physical and aesthetic properties of graphic materials
- joining materials
- 'smart' and modern materials
- environmental and sustainability issues.

Design:

- the generation of ideas
- the evaluation and modification of ideas
- function and aesthetics
- modelling of design proposals
- justification for choice and rejection of ideas
- selection and justification of materials
- understanding the purpose of prototyping
- applying ergonomic and anthropometric data.

Product planning:

- choosing and preparing materials
- planning work.

Tools and equipment:

- basic graphic materials equipment.

Processes:

- recognise, name and draw basic graphic shapes and developments
- read, interpret and produce drawings to scale
- use of enhancement techniques
- graphical interpretation of data
- developments
- the conversion or altering of materials into other usable forms
- manufacturing processes
- printing methods
- cutting and creasing
- mechanical systems.

Computer applications:

- use of CAD packages
- on-screen modelling
- storing and sharing data
- application of CAD/CAM to making models, one-off and quantity production
- computer control of machines (CNC)
- copyright issues
- selection of appropriate text styles for a given situation
- use of image manipulation software
- vector and bitmap images.

Health and safety:

- the importance of health and safety
- basic risk assessment
- the importance of following instructions
- recognising and understanding safety symbols.

Quality:

- distinguish between quality of design and quality of manufacture
- how the quality of a product may be affected by materials and processes
- the marks and symbols used on packaging to inform consumers about quality
- describe simple quality control checks.

Product analysis:

- establish the function of commercially manufactured products
- determine the intended market or users for a product
- identify materials and components from which products are made
- identify the processes used to make the product

- compare products designed to meet the same need
- assess commercially manufactured products and identify improvements
- evaluate commercially manufactured products against moral, cultural, environmental and sustainability issues
- carry out a life cycle analysis (LCA) of a variety of products.

KEY TERM

CONTENT – body of information you need to know in order to sit the exam

11.4 HOW TO PREPARE FOR THE EXAM

LEARNING OUTCOME

By the end of this section you should have developed a knowledge and understanding of:

- how to prepare for this unit exam.

*The best way to **prepare** for the exam for this unit is through focused practical tasks, and designing and making assignments.*

Figure 11.2 Designing and making assignments

▶ Preparation for the exam

In this unit, you should develop your knowledge and understanding through:

- designing and making
- focused practical tasks
- specific theory lessons.

These tasks will vary in nature – some will be based around group discussion, others will involve working with ideas and media, **researching** concepts and recording information. Activities may also involve visits to particular technology innovation centres, museums and industry. Your teacher will decide how to combine these activities to produce an exciting and interesting course.

Evidence should be collected and recorded, and can be used at the end of the unit for exam preparation.

1	Paper	
2	Card & board	
3	Thin sheet plastics	✓
4	'Smart' & modern materials	
5	Rigid foam & balsa wood	✓
6	Joining materials	✓
7	Finishing materials	
8	Standard pre-manufactured components	

Figure 11.3 Covering the content

KEY POINTS

- Preparation for the unit exam should be through a series of designing and making tasks, focused practical tasks and theory lessons.
- Over time, these activities will build up your knowledge and understanding of the technical aspects.

EXAMINER'S TIPS

- Keep a record of the activities you have undertaken.
- Record what you have done or found out in each of the activities.
- Use a tick list to check you have covered the content.

KEY TERMS

PREPARE – to get ready
RESEARCH – collecting and analysing information

11.5 THE EXAM

LEARNING OUTCOMES

By the end of this section you should have developed a knowledge and understanding of:

- the exam structure
- the types of question that will be asked.

 This unit is worth 20% of the total marks for the full GCSE course. It is externally assessed.

The exam structure

This unit is assessed by a 75-minute exam that is divided into section A and section B. The paper will consist of five questions that focus on technical aspects of designing and making. Each question is worth 12 marks. The mark available for each part of a question is shown in square brackets [ ].

The quality of written communication is assessed in this unit.

Section A

Section A consists of three questions based on the technical aspects of working with materials, tools and equipment. Examples of section A questions are shown below.

An example of a section A question

One surface of the development (net) required to make a model train has been drawn below.

Complete the development (net) by adding:

(i) the other five surfaces [5]

(ii) the glue tabs. [1]

Do not show any of the surface detail.

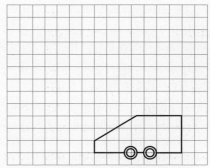

Full size development (net) of model train

Figure 11.4 Development (net) of model train

Mark scheme

(i) The other five surfaces:

- Top and back correctly positioned [1]
- Second side correctly positioned [1]
- Wheels added [1]
- Sloping surface and front correctly positioned [1]
- Majority of sizes are correct. [1]

(ii) The glue tabs:

- At least four workable glue flaps correctly added. [1]

An example of a section A question

Discuss how the production of a printed ticket for an athletics event could take into account environmental issues. [6]

Mark scheme

- **Level 1 (0–2 marks):** Basic discussion, showing limited understanding of environmental issues to consider. There will be little or no use of specialist terms. Answers may be ambiguous or disorganised. Errors of grammar, punctuation and spelling may be intrusive.

- **Level 2 (3–4 marks):** Adequate discussion, showing some understanding of the environmental issues to consider and how they can take account of them. There will be some use of specialist terms, although these may not always be used appropriately. The information will be presented for the most part in a structured format. There may be occasional errors in spelling, grammar and punctuation.

- **Level 3 (5–6 marks):** Thorough discussion, showing detailed understanding of the environmental issues to consider and how they can take account of them. Specialist terms used appropriately and correctly. The information is presented in a structured format. The candidate demonstrates accurate spelling, punctuation and grammar.

The discussion could include:

- more complex shapes create waste material, then the manufacturer has to dispose of the waste

- shapes that tessellate

- how the ticket is printed

- nature of the chemicals used in the print process

- material the ticket is produced from.

Section B

Section B consists of two questions on the design of products, reflecting the wider aspects of sustainability and human use. One of these questions will require a design response. An example of section B question is shown below.

An example of a section B question

A set of stamps will be issued to commemorate a sporting event. Each stamp is to illustrate a different athletics event. The design to be used on the stamp showing running events is shown in Figure 11.5. The other stamps are to show similar stylised athletes.

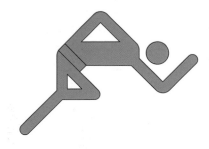

Figure 11.5 Stylised athlete to be used on running events stamp

(a) Develop a design for a stamp based on the following specification. The stamp must feature one of the following events:

(i)   shot put

(ii) long jump

(iii) javelin

(iv) hurdles.

The design must include a stylised drawing of an athlete involved in the event that you have chosen. [3]

Figure 11.6 Design resource material

Mark scheme

The design must include a stylised drawing of an athlete involved in an event.

- Design has been developed using notes and several sketches. [1]
- Design shows some attempt to stylise chosen athlete. [1]
- A good stylised design has been produced. [1]

INDEX